A HISTORY OF THEATRICAL ART

A History of Theatrical Art

In Ancient and Modern Times by

Karl Mantzius

With an Introduction by William Archer

Authorised Translation by

Louise von Cossel

Volume I

The Earliest Times

GLOUCESTER, MASS.

PETER SMITH

1970

First Published, 1903
Reprinted, 1937
Reprinted, 1970

CONTENTS

CONTENTS

LIST OF ILLUSTRATIONS

INTRODUCTION

DR KARL MANTZIUS, the author of this *History of Theatrical Art*, is one of the few actors of note who have also won distinction in the field of serious scholarship. It is by no means uncommon for actors—even apart from the supreme instances of Shakespeare and Molière—to possess a considerable share of literary talent. David Garrick cut no contemptible figure in the brilliant literary society of his day. John Philip Kemble and Macready were both men of parts and reading. In our own day, by the courtesy of journalism, all actor-managers are "scholarly," just as all Homer's Greeks are "well-greaved"; but the tangible results of their scholarship are not very apparent. In any case, however ardent their passion for research, the time they can devote to it is necessarily limited. The actor's calling, even without the additional responsibilities of management, is a most exacting one; so that anything like erudition is very rarely to be expected of him. A great part, at any rate, of the literary work of Louis Riccoboni was done after his retirement from the stage; and Eduard Devrient, when he wrote his *History of German Acting*, was not, I take it, actively engaged in his profession. It is difficult, then, to find a parallel case to that of Dr Mantzius, who, while holding a leading position in the Royal Theatre of Copenhagen, and constantly employed both as actor and stage-manager, has found time to produce, not a paste-and-scissor compilation, such as many actors have lent their names to, but a well-ordered work of thoroughly competent scholarship.

It need scarcely be said that Dr Mantzius had the groundwork of a solid literary education to build upon. He was born in 1860, the son of a distinguished actor at the Royal Theatre, who died in 1879. At the University of Copenhagen and in Paris, young Mantzius studied the philology and literature of the Romance Languages. He began life as a journalist and teacher; but the hereditary bias was too strong for him, and in 1883 he joined the company of the Royal Theatre. This institution, founded about the middle of the eighteenth century by the great comedy-writer, Ludvig Holberg, is surpassed by the Comédie Française alone in the antiquity and splendour of its associations. Mantzius began his stage career as a comic actor and "raisonneur" in modern plays, and at first made his way but slowly, because he would not give in to the prevailing fashion of over-emphasis in comedy and declamation in drama. During the past ten years, however, he has unquestionably become one of the three or four leading artists of the company, his position as a tragedian and character-actor being equivalent to that of Olaf Poulsen as a comedian. Harpagon, in Molière's *L'Avare*, may be said to have bridged for him the gap between the comic and the tragic domains. It led him on to Shakespeare's Richard III.—a part which he "created" so far as the Danish stage was concerned—to Shylock, and to King Lear. He has also acted many of the leading parts in the plays of Henrik Ibsen—such as Bishop Nicholas in *The Pretenders*, Daniel Heire in *The League of Youth*, Helmer in *A Doll's House*, Dr Relling in *The Wild Duck*, and Brack in *Hedda Gabler*. He is most popular in modern character-parts, though he confesses that his predilection is for the classics.

In 1901 Mantzius took the degree of *Doctor Philosophiae* at the University of Copenhagen. This was no honorary distinction such as several universities have conferred (for example) on Sir Henry Irving. Mantzius "proceeded doctor" in the ordinary way, by presenting a dissertation, and "defending" it in open session of the Philosophic Faculty. His dissertation was the History of the English Theatre in the time of Shakespeare, which forms the third volume of the present work.

It will be observed that Dr Mantzius does not profess to write a history of the Drama, but of "Theatrical Art." In other words, he studies literary developments only in so far as they are affected by, and in their turn react upon, the actual processes of representation. He takes up mimetic art, indeed, at a period long antecedent to the construction of regular theatres. He seeks out its germs among savage races, and compares the phases of its evolution among widely - separated peoples. And to this task he brings, not only diligent and comprehensive study, but a practical knowledge of the conditions of theatrical representation in which too many of the scholars who have dealt with the history of ancient, mediæval and Renaissance drama have been obviously deficient. Numberless errors and absurdities have gained currency in theatrical history, because the documents (literary, graphic and architectural), from which alone the theatres of bygone ages can be reconstructed, have been interpreted by writers who had no clear imaginative realisation of the fundamental laws—the inherent possibilities and impossibilities—of theatrical art. There has been a marked tendency of late, in England, France and Germany, towards what may be called realism in the study of stage history. It has been recognised that the merits and limitations of the drama of the past can be but imperfectly apprehended until we understand, not only the civilisation of the public to which it appealed, but the actual methods and mechanism of its presentation. In order thoroughly to master the Attic drama, we must place ourselves, in imagination, in the Theatre of Dionysus; if we are not radically to misconstrue some of the most characteristic features of Shakespeare's art, we must frequent in spirit the Globe and the Blackfriars Playhouses of his day. Dr Mantzius's work is a very important outcome of this realistic tendency in modern dramatic criticism. It is evident that, if an actor possesses the necessary scholarship, he stands in a position of peculiar advantage for vividly and intelligently reconstructing the bygone manifestations of his art. That Dr Mantzius has made excellent use of the advantages of his position will be doubted by no one who reads his well-informed, well-ordered, lucid and suggestive chapters.

WILLIAM ARCHER.

INTRODUCTION

I

The Relation of Dramatic Art to other Arts.

THERE is in human nature a tendency to reproduce and communicate to others the impressions received from the surrounding world; indeed, the manifestation of such impressions is the basis of every kind of art.

We shall see that, from this point of view, the domain of art is large, yet sharply defined. In every human being there is a primitive capacity for artistic production; everybody is capable to a certain degree of receiving and reproducing impressions, and it is this universal innate gift that lends art its greatest importance.

After all, there is no difference of kind between the image of a man or woman drawn by a child on its slate and the statue of the Venus of Milo; both reveal the artistic power of communicating impressions produced by surrounding objects on the human mind. If we do not dignify the child's attempt by the name of art, it is only because the impression it imparts is so infinitely weak compared with the mighty effect produced by the mature art of a fully-developed man. They differ only in degree, not in kind, while there is an essential difference between a photograph, however excellent, and an image drawn by the human hand. A photograph may reproduce nature with much more accurate outlines than a work of art, yet all it can do is to present the impres-

sion of an object on a glass plate; among the many processes through which human ingenuity makes it pass, it
just misses the one which would have raised it to the
level of art, and which goes on in the *camera obscura* of
the human mind.

While thus, on the one hand, a work of art must
originate in an impression on the human brain,[1] on the
other, the capacity of reproducing this impression and
imparting it to others is a factor at least equally important.   Let a person possess the most delicate sensi-
bility to impressions, but at the same time—if possible
—be quite devoid of the power of reproduction, and
he is absolutely incapable of creating art.   Lessing's
paradox about Raphael: "Do you think, Prince, that
Raphael would have been the greatest painter, even if
he had been unfortunate enough to be born without
hands?"[2] is senseless, unless we suppose that man is born
under predestination with fully developed artistic capacity;
and in that case we might as well alter the sentence and
say: "Do you think Raphael would have been the
greatest painter, even if by a misfortune he had been
born blind?"

It is even essentially on *reproduction*, on the com-
munication to others, that the accent must be laid, if we
want to give a clear definition of the nature of art; for,
while the gift of reproduction necessarily presupposes
that of reception, the reverse is not the case.   All the
higher animals, for instance, are quite capable of receiv-

---

[1] Compare Zola's well-known definition of a work of art : "Un coin de
nature, vu à travers un tempérament."

[2] *Emilia Galotti*, Act II., Sc. 4.

ing impressions of the outer world similar to our own, but very few of them are able to express them in a way which at all resembles what we call art, viz., to call forth feelings corresponding to those of the communicator. The songs of birds are no doubt a kind of primitive art; the bird sings in memory of the pleasures and pangs of love it has felt : is not this what we call music?

While we measure the power of art by the impression it produces on ourselves—all appreciation of art is and must be individual—we divide its branches according to its different modes of manifestation. If it expresses itself by sounds, we call it music; if by colours, painting; if by form, sculpture; if by steps and gestures, dancing; if by verse, poetry; if by spoken words combined with gesture, acting.

It is clear, however, that these different branches, whose domains now appear so sharply limited, did not in the beginning spring into existence fully developed; art had to grope its way and to work on for thousands of years, before its different modes of expression evolved into independent branches, each with a purpose of its own. For instance, we easily understand that music, dancing, acting and poetry were originally combined, none of them existing in the shape which characterises it at present. Among peoples who stood on a low level of civilisation, these arts worked collectively in shouting, singing, acting, talking and jumping.

Only by degrees and quite slowly did the art of tones detach itself and develop into music, and steps, gambols and gestures form themselves into regular dances. The arts of poetry and acting probably remained combined

longer than any others, and naturally enough : the first
who arranged his words artistically in order to express
his sorrow or his joy and to make others weep or laugh,
did not think that anybody but himself would make use
of these words, and he sang or recited them as best
he might.   But later, when the artist, not finding it
sufficient to picture his own feelings, but wishing to
reproduce those of others as well, introduced several
individuals, each speaking for himself, dramatic art
developed into an independent branch with a purpose of
its own.

II

The First Germs of Dramatic Art—Dancing and its Use in the Service of
Religion—Secret Societies among Uncivilised Nations—Disguises
and Mummeries.

If we wish to trace the first movements of dramatic art,
and to see under what forms and circumstances its
earliest germs developed, we naturally refer to accounts
of the amusements and festivals of the savage nations,
next to the semi-barbarous tribes whose development
stopped at a very early stage, and finally to the nations
of whose extinct civilisation there are accounts extant.

What strikes us first of all in making these researches
is the astonishing uniformity in the first germs and
earliest development of dramatic representation, even in
peoples so far removed from each other, geographically
and ethnographically, that a mutual influence and imitation must be considered out of the question.   It is
interesting to notice that the Greek drama—so poetical
and perfect in form—does not differ essentially from the

religious festivals of the Indians of the North-West, or
that the masques and farces which are still performed in
civilised Europe find analogies, for instance, among the
Melanesian peoples, inhabitants of the South Sea Islands.
We have set ourselves the task of first of all pointing
out some fundamental features in the earliest stage of
dramatic art, during which all nations may be treated
nearly alike, and of subsequently giving an account of
the forms of acting in use among some nations of more
advanced civilisation.

By investigating the artistic phenomena of primitive
tribes we find our above-stated supposition confirmed,
viz., that their artistic aspirations manifested themselves
in a mixture of the four arts : music, dancing, acting and
poetry. Out of this combination of subsequently distinct
forms of art, however, dancing seems to have been the
first which developed itself into an accepted expression
of certain emotions, thus becoming a kind of art. Dancing, indeed, is in its origin nothing but involuntary
movements of the body reflecting the joyful emotions
of the mind. When the heart is heavy and sad the
body is unnerved, the muscles become flabby, the
limbs will droop ; but as soon as the soul is stirred by
a sudden impulse of joy or passion, the body at
once feels lighter, the muscles will strain themselves,
and the limbs stir—quite instinctively. Indeed, the
capers of a happy child indicate the spontaneous origin
of the art of dancing.

Now, as in peoples of rudimentary culture religious
feeling is the highest form of emotion, it is natural that
dancing, being the most expressive way of exhibiting

this emotion, was everywhere taken into the service of religion, first as an involuntary expression of increased excitement, later as a symbol.   We see, in fact, that the lowest primitive nations, who have no religious ideas to speak of, or only such simple and poor ones that religious worship is out of the question, have no dancing either; while, on the other hand, the peoples to whom dramatic acting is entirely unknown, perform dances at a few of their religious ceremonies.   The Patagonians, whose only religious feelings consist in a panic horror of evil spirits, and who possess no sacred cult whatever, limit their dancing and poetry—if such expressions can be used at all—to a monotonous mumbling of senseless incantations, accompanied by a perpetual rocking of the body.   On these occasions they mask themselves in a primitive way by daubing their heads with chalk.   This seems to be the most rudimentary form of dancing.

But even among the Australians we already find the commencements of ritual ceremonies with dances, in which the performers appear fantastically decked out with flowers, feathers and wreaths, and their skin greased and covered with white clay.   These dances are usually performed at night by torchlight, but we do not know anything of their real character; they are considered as religious mysteries, and as such kept strictly secret from strangers.   The painting of the skin and the peculiar disguise no doubt have something to do with the mystic character of the dances, and most likely were adopted in order to prevent the dancers from being recognised; for it is a common feature with otherwise most diverse nations that the performers of sacred

1—Masks used in scenes of disguise by secret societies (North America).

ceremonies disguise themselves in some way by paint and masks. Among the Aleutians, for instance, mystic mask-dances form part of their holy ceremonies ; some of these dances are performed exclusively by women, others exclusively by men. Hundreds of naked women dance round their idols by moonlight, and all have their faces covered with wooden masks painted in imitation of heads of sea animals. These masks have no apertures for the eyes, only holes beneath the nose, which allow the bearers to look downward, but in no other direction.

In their religious worship the American Indians also know of mystic festivals at which whole pantomimes are performed and the actors appear disguised, especially as animals, and belong to secret societies (fig. 1). No outsider was admitted to these strictly ritual dances. Secret societies are also a constantly recurring and peculiar feature of the worship of savage nations. For one thing, their original purpose seems to have been to practise dances and plays which were to be performed at religious festivals. The time of apprenticeship, as a rule, was long and severe, and it was by no means everybody who could be admitted into these societies. On the other hand, their members enjoyed particular privileges. Thus the *Hamatsa* among the North-West Indians were allowed to eat human flesh ; a prerogative, however, which advanced civilisation has so far reduced that this corporation, which still exists, must limit its appetite to corpses.

Among the different tribes on the South Sea Islands secret societies are widely spread under different names, as *Quatu* on the New Hebrides, *Tamate* on the Banks Islands (fig. 2), *Matambala* on the Solomon Islands,

Duk-Duk in New Britain, and finally the power-ful corporation of the *Areoi*, which extends all over Polynesia.

Common features of all these societies are: the mystery which surrounds them ; their religious origin and their agency ; dancing. What enables them to keep up their mysterious character is the inflexible severity with which they exclude outsiders from their meetings. Thus the Duk-Duks mercilessly kill and eat anybody who may happen—even inadvertently—to intrude on their proceed-ings. Their dances, which differ very much in character, though no doubt they are all of religious origin, are indeed performed in public, but always under disguise and generally with masked faces (fig. 3). Here also the masks serve the purpose of concealment and mystifica-tion ; they belong to the religious cult and are not meant to indicate the character of the figure. As a rule they are quite fantastic, representing either monstrous animal heads or—most frequently — grotesque human figures ; they generally cover the whole head like the Greek masks, and, if so, the faces are carved of light wood and gaudily painted in red, black and white ; the head is covered with a framework of cane, decorated with vegetable substances to represent hair. Sometimes the masks are made of two tortoise shells put together, elaborately carved and joined with shells (fig. 5). In New Britain a particular kind of mask is used : each dancer takes a skull of one of his deceased relatives, of which he makes a mask for his face, providing it at the back with a transverse bar, which he keeps between his teeth while dancing. The head is covered with a kind

2—Member of a secret society in mumming-dress (Tamate), Banks Islands.
3—Fantastic masks (North America).   4—Skull masks from New Britain.

of clay painted with red, white and blue stripes round eyes and mouth (fig. 4).

The Areoi, however, the most distinguished of all these societies, use no masks at all; they content themselves with painting their faces red and their bodies black. This strange society, which in several respects reminds us of still-existing European corporations, consists of seven degrees, into the uppermost of which not even princes of high rank disdain to enter. Each degree possesses its steadily increasing privileges and its particular tattooing, except the seventh and lowest, which does not use tattooing properly so called, and is laid under an obligation to perform the ritual dances and ceremonies wherever the society appears. The Areoi used to go in boats decorated with flowers from one island to another, where small temples were erected in honour of the god Oros. They were welcomed with respectful joy by the islanders; and, as long as they remained, performed their dances and pantomimes, which in the beginning were of a religious character, but afterwards became historical and comical. The spectators were deeply impressed with these grotesque entertainments, in which vehement gesticulations were accompanied by a queer kind of music.—Is not this indeed the original type of a touring company of actors?

In all nations, civilised as well as primitive, religious and symbolic dances have formed part of the divine service. Even some of the most serious peoples and those who showed least aptitude for mimic art, such as the Egyptians, Turks and Jews, all knew dancing. Jewish history, for instance, which nowhere shows the slightest trace of dramatic literature or art, tells us of David's dancing before the Ark, and of the Israelitish women who danced out to meet Saul, as well as of the standing ceremony of jumping up high three times after certain prayers, as a symbolic sign that the soul had left the body and ascended to God.[1] This, as well as other similar customs, was kept up in the Christian service, in which, as we know, dancing is still used among the agencies of the Roman Catholic Church.

III

Mimic Dances—Erotic Subjects—Imitation of Animals—Mimic Representation of Everyday Occupations—War Dances—The Historical Pantomime and its Comic Interlude.

By degrees, as the symbolic signification of dancing extends to direct imitation of nature, it loses its purely lyrical character; the dramatic element is introduced, and it becomes mimical. Among peoples with some culture mimic dances are known from the earliest times side by side with religious dances, but no doubt the latter were the origin of the former. The most common subject, which, so to say, lay immediately at hand and which everybody could understand, man's ever youthful desire to win woman's love, recurs in ever-varying form in innumerable *pas de deux*. Erotic dances where the man woos, the woman refuses, teases, excites and finally yields, were performed among the most diverse nations, among some with graceful and decent indication of the desire, but as a rule with a naïve cynicism which

[1] Buxdorf: *Synagoga judaica*, chap. x. p. 207, quoted by Ed. du Méril : *La Comédie ancienne*, i. p. 66.

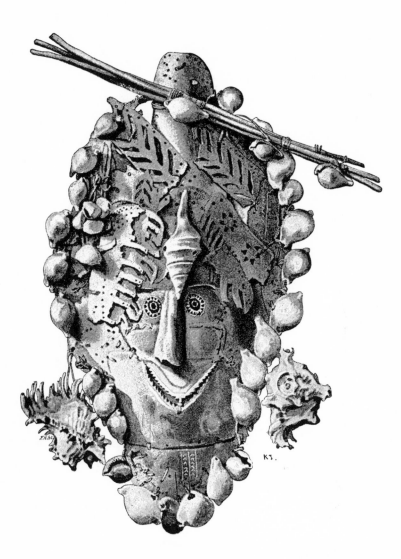

5—Tortoise mask, Murray Islands (Melanesian).

converted mimic art into unveiled reality. The Greeks
danced their *Kordax* with such gross licentiousness that
it was considered a disgrace to take part in it without
being either masked or drunk.[1] Among the natives in
central America the Spaniards found mimic erotic dances
which reminded them of those of their home country ;
the performers—at least on some occasions—seemed to
have intoxicated themselves with a kind of snuff. In the
South Sea Islands, too, obscene pairing dances were
performed under different names (*Ehura, Mamma, Mem-
mah-pepeh*), and the Areoi had several erotic scenes in
their list of performances.

Out of the first germ of dramatic art, which, we may
say, lies hidden in this little mimic dance, and gradually
as imitation of nature becomes more and more a favourite
entertainment, other scenes grow up and are added to
the above-described ; all are quite plain, containing a
simple subject easily understood by everybody. One of
the earliest and most widely spread of these motives is
the imitation of animals. Even in their dances primitive
peoples were fond of copying the appearance and movements of animals, at first only by peculiar attitudes and
gestures. We see, for instance, that the Australians, in
their hunting dances, are capable of imitating the peculiarities of the emu, the kangaroo, the frog, and other
animals, merely by movements, especially with their
arms, by which they represent the neck either of the
emu or of the kangaroo. Later they deck themselves
out also either with the hide or feathers of the animal
in question, and make masks which, in a more or less

---

[1] Theophrastus' *Characters*, chap. vi.

fantastic way, represent heads of birds or other animals ;
they even cover their skin with imperishable tattooings.
The red Indians in particular excel in these animal
disguises ; their bear, dog, and buffalo dances are said to
be more like pantomimic farces than like what we call
dances (fig. 6). Their dramatic point consists in making
a comical chase after the supposed animals, some of the
dancers representing the hunters, others the beasts.

This kind of imitation, which in the beginning probably
afforded sufficient pleasure in itself, recurs in all nations
at a certain stage of their civilisation. Sometimes it
consists in grotesque fights, sometimes in regular dances,
in which the manners of animals are mimicked. These
performances have survived down to our own times in
certain national customs and popular games. The
sounds of the beasts were copied as well as their movements, and in the delight with which this art is still
cultivated as a remarkable accomplishment we recognise
the first elements of the sense of rhythm.

In the course of time, as the different branches of
industry grew up, it was found interesting and stimulating to see everyday work idealised and characterised by
gestures and choregraphic signs representing the professional movements of the different trades. Thus a
kind of industrial pantomime was created. All the
occupations which could be easily represented by fixed
movements were arranged into ballets. The *blacksmith's
dances*, for instance, illustrated the swinging of the
sledge-hammer by the smith ; the *fishing dances* imitated
by conventional rhythmic movements the rocking of a
boat on the waves and the sweeping of the seine.

6—Indian animal disguise.   A Shaman as a bear.

Imitative dances of this kind have also survived in the popular games of European nations. We quote some examples from " Kindergarten Songs and Games." [1]

THE WOODMEN.

We're the woodmen, busy sawing,
'Neath the trees where rooks are cawing,
Sawing, sawing, see-saw see;
Short and thin bits,
Long and thick bits,
See-saw, see-saw, see-saw see.

A. B.

Two rows of children face each other, each child joining hands across with its opposite neighbour. The left arms represent the wood and the right arms the saw. The sawing is done strictly in time to the singing, and at " See-saw " in the last line the time is doubled.

THE PEASANT.[2]

I

Shall we show you how the peasant,
In the spring and autumn pleasant,
With their show'rs and sunshine present,
Sows the corn for our food?
See! 'tis so, so that the peasant,
In the spring and autumn pleasant,
With their show'rs and sunshine present,
Sows the corn for our food.
La, la, la, la, la, la, la, la.

[1] Edited by Mrs E. Berry and Mme. Michaelis of the Froebel Society. Published by W. Shepherd.
[2] Folk-song.

2

Shall we show you how the peasant,
Watched by partridge and by pheasant,
When September days are pleasant,
      Reaps the corn for our food ?
See! 'tis so, etc.

3

Shall we show you how the peasant,
How the hot and thirsty peasant,
With his team and waggon present,
      Carries corn for our food ?
See! 'tis so, etc.

4

Shall we show you how the peasant,
When no steam-machine is present
To relieve his toil unpleasant,
      Threshes corn for our food ?
See! 'tis so, etc.

5

Shall we show you how the peasant,
How the worn-out honest peasant,
With contentment in the present,
      Rests when labour's done ?
See! 'tis so, etc.

6

Shall we show you how the peasant,
At the Harvest Home so pleasant,

> With the men and master present,
>   Sports when labour's done?
> See! 'tis so, etc.

The whole of the children stand in a circle, and imitate the actions of the peasant from the words, "See! 'tis so, etc," in each verse. To form the waggons the children divide into pairs, and run one behind the other, holding hands.

5th Verse.—This is sung quietly, the children sitting on their heels, resting the right elbow on their knee, and their head on their hand.

6th Verse.—The children dance round in couples.

At "La, la, la" in each verse the circle dances round to the time of the song.

Nor was war, the chief delight of savage nations, forgotten. Next to religious dances war-dances were probably the most important festive ceremonies among these peoples. They were divided into two kinds : those which were performed before the war, and had for their essential purpose to excite the courage and ferocity of the fighters (the Iroquois, by-the-bye, prepared themselves for every important undertaking by seizing their weapons, knocking their tomahawks against each other with rhythmic movements, and threatening each other with their spears) ;[1] and those which followed when peace had been concluded, commemorating the war as an event which was happily brought to a close. To the latter category belongs the *Korrobboree* of the Australians, of which Bahnson gives the following description:[2] "Several

---

[1] E. du Méril : *op. cit.*
[2] Kr. Bahnson : *Antropologie der Naturvölker,* i. p. 34 f.

tribes are wont to assemble for this festival, which is held by moonlight. The day before the appointed date the men remain concealed in the bushes, in order to decorate themselves for the festival by rubbing their skin thoroughly with grease and covering it with white clay. Towards sunset the women light a great fire and strike up a monotonous song, in which the same verse is constantly repeated ; they accompany it by beating on a piece of opossum-hide, stretched on their knees like a drum-skin, or by knocking together two boomerangs (wooden missiles used by the Australians in war and hunting). Armed with clubs, spears and other weapons, or swinging torches, the men rush out from among the bushes. Conducted by a man who beats the time with two sticks or clubs, they begin their dance by winding and twisting their bodies, stamping on the ground, and making all kinds of gestures and grimaces. From time to time their lines dissolve into a confused crowd ; small groups play a game which consists in chasing each other in a circle, running backwards and forwards till the lines close again and dancing begins afresh. This goes on throughout the night till the following morning." From this description, as well as from the illustration (fig. 7), we see distinctly that this dance really consists of a series of symbolic movements taken from war customs; the small groups playing " catch " are evidently mimicking enemies who fight with alternating success.

The Red Indians knew another kind of war-dance, which was also performed when peace had been made ; this dance, strangely enough, was executed by women.

C·H·F·S.

7—The Korrobboree (Australian war-dance).

It was the so-called *scalp-dance*. While the medicine-men—*Shamans*—sing and mark the rhythm on their primitive musical instruments, the women—painted red and decorated with beads and ribbons—dance in concentric circles round the scalps, which are suspended on a pole in the centre; sometimes one of the women carries them on her shoulder. At each stroke on the drum the dancers rise on tiptoe, jump up and slide a little to the left, all the time singing in perfect rhythm with the music of the *Shamans*. After some minutes the women have to rest. During this pause one of them relates events of the past war, especially the deeds and deaths of the fallen men; at last she exclaims: " Whose scalps do I now carry on my shoulder?" At these words they all jump up again with cheers and screams of vengeance, and dancing begins afresh. Sometimes this goes on for months, with intervals between the performances. We notice with interest the recitals intermixed with these scalp-dances. In fact, we stand here at the threshold of the real drama, the origin of which—in Greece, for instance —will be found to be quite similar to this Indian dance. If the interspersed tales about the heroes, instead of being told by one person, were put into the mouths of several actors, thus giving a graphic representation of the facts as they had happened, or were supposed to have happened, the drama would have been there.

This threshold, however, of the great edifice of the drama and the art of acting, no primitive people was able to pass. The Incas perhaps possessed real dramatic literature, but this people had a comparatively high civilisation, which, strictly speaking, placed it beyond and above the primitive nations; nor does it seem impossible that their plays (either of a domestic homely kind or real historical tragedies) had been influenced by European culture, or that the specimens preserved may have been, consciously or unconsciously, altered by the Europeans who made them known.[1]

The more primitive nations took another course; instead of the drama they created the *historical pantomime*.

A people need not be very old to have a history of which certain great events are commemorated on their recurring anniversaries; but in the course of time the younger generations lose sight of these festivals, and it becomes necessary to revive the memory of them by processions, dances, mimic representations, etc., the drift of which is the illustration of past historical facts.   Thus—thousands of years ago—in memory of their ancestors' wanderings in the desert, the Jews celebrated the Feast of *Tabernacles*; and though now they are scattered over the whole globe and have ceased to be an independent nation, this feast is still commemorated wherever they live.   In Alsace, for instance, the orthodox Jews build arbours in which they spend the seven days this festival lasts.[2]   Out of these commemorative festivals the historical pantomime arose quite naturally.   It was probably common to most of the now existing civilised nations, and is still celebrated with great pomp and splendour by many exotic peoples; it is probably the highest display of their dramatic art.   The Polynesian Areoi, in addition

---

[1] Two Inca plays have survived: one, called *Ollanta*, a historical drama of passion, is complete; of the other, entitled *Usca Pancar*, only a fragment remains, and its genuineness is contested.

[2] E. du Méril: *op. cit.* i.

to their obscenely erotic dances, perform very long pantomimes, the subjects of which are drawn from legendary
lore. The Siamese, Chinese and Japanese show considerable art, and display great scenic apparatus in their
pantomimes. Before coming under European influence
the Siamese were unacquainted with any other form of
drama, whereas in China and Japan the pantomime
flourished side by side with a comparatively well developed dramatic art. In Japan, as in the old English
drama, dumb show was frequently mingled with the
recited scenes.

It seems to be a strong point with the Japanese to
interpret very passionate feelings through dumb show
only. In an ancient book of travels the following description is found : " Some of their performances consist
of dances and the representation of various emotions like
that which in former times was exhibited by the Roman
pantomimes. The dancers do not speak, but by means
of costumes, action and gesticulation accompanied by
music, they make it their object to represent the plot
in the most natural way. The principal accessories of
the stage, such as wells, bridges, gates, houses, gardens,
mountains or animals, are represented as naturally as
possible, and are so contrived that, just as on the European stage, they can instantly be removed or taken to
pieces at a given signal.

" The actresses are generally young girls who get
their training in houses of ill-fame, and the actors are
boys from the street where the play is performed,
and whose inhabitants pay the expenses of it. As a
rule they wear magnificent dresses suitable to their parts,

and deserve praise for the boldness and grace of their acting, which is scarcely equalled by European players."[1] Though this account is somewhat vague, and though several points in it, for instance the description of the stage, require explanation (which will be found in the subsequent section about Japan), the author lays particular emphasis on the great superiority of the Japanese in dumb show. A similar judgment is pronounced by a modern traveller, Dr. Hermann Maron.[2] He says : "One thing in particular strikes me in their theatrical performances—the frequent intermixture of the drama with dumb show. . . . Where the passions culminate, dumb show is resorted to, . . . such emotions as anger, jealousy or agony being rendered in the minutest details, with as much subtlety and perfection as I have ever seen on an imperial or royal stage in Europe. In some of them I particularly admired a surprisingly delicate action of the hands. . . ."

Sometimes also the pathetic parts of the play are interrupted by simple dances or rhythmic choregraphic figures,[3] which in a direct way remind one of the origin of the drama.

In China dumb show is not mixed up with the drama ; it forms a separate branch of art, or rather an entertainment which has nothing to do with the particular way in which dramatic art has developed. It

---

[1] Engelbrecht Kämpfer : *Geschichte und Beschreibung von Japan.* Kämpfer was a famous physician and traveller, who lived at the close of the seventeenth and the beginning of the eighteenth century.

[2] *Japan und China*, Berlin, 1863, I.

[3] George Bousquet : *Le Théâtre au Japon.* (*Revue des deux Mondes*, 1874, July-August.)

might most fitly be compared with the lifeless productions manufactured by European managers of circus
and variety performances, in which the principal stress
is laid on the staging and the mechanical *tours
d'adresse*, while the plot is only an indifferent framework. Lord Macartney in his diary describes a pantomime which was performed at the conclusion of a great
festival given in his honour by the Emperor of China.
The subject was : The Wedding of the Ocean with the
Earth. Bride and bridegroom—sea and earth—poured
out their treasures before the eyes of the spectators,
and the most frightful monsters from the wet and dry
realms danced round on the stage and at last placed
themselves in two rows in order to make room for the
whale, the king of all monsters. This animal then
waddled down to the foreground, where it squirted out
barrels of water towards the imperial box, as a delicate
attention to the distinguished guest who was sitting
there. It must be observed that the floor of the box
was pierced with holes, so as to make the water run
out at once. This final effect was hailed with a thunder
of applause by the select assembly. Some mandarins of
the first class and distinguished courtiers who were seated
with Lord Macartney, were in raptures, and repeatedly
exclaimed : " Hao, hung hao ! admirable ! splendid !
celestial ! " [1] After all, is there much difference between
this enthusiasm, which at first strikes us as ridiculous, and
the transport of our select public at water-pantomimes
and other wonders of the circus? The pure and
unsophisticated historical pantomime which flourished

[1] *Life of the Earl of Macartney,* vol. ii. p. 156.

so admirably in our own country[1] during this century has probably never been surpassed anywhere. Bournonville's[2] national ballets are precisely a modern revival of this primitive form of art ; perhaps we may say that it culminated in these works through the artistic finish, the poetic and ingenious mimic art which formed their principal attraction.

Compared with these conscious works of art, the attempts of the oriental nations naturally appear rude and elementary. Their imagination was incapable of mastering the extensive historical matter, so they reproduced it with a childish and minute attention to unimportant details, which we think fatiguing and quite inartistic. Therefore their performances — after the fashion of mediæval mysteries — sometimes went on for months. Nor could they distinguish illusion from reality ; from a mistaken realistic tendency (which, by-the-bye, is not quite unknown even in our own days), they performed everything with a naïve accuracy and reality which left nothing for the imagination to do. If, for instance, the play prescribed that horsemen should gallop across the stage and run away, this was actually done by riders on living horses, and the spectators felt satisfied that all was real and no sham. In a Siamese play the desire for reality went so far that, after the actors had left the stage, all the women undressed and took their bath.[3] In the play they were said to be alone, so there was no need to be ashamed of their nudity.

---

[1] Denmark.   [2] A Danish *maître de ballet*, 1805-79.
[3] Bowring : *Kingdom and People of Siam*, ii. p. 326.

The long historical plays with their solemn heroic subjects naturally became fatiguing even to so naïve a public as the primitive nations, and the idea arose of relieving the supreme monotony of the representations by comical *interludes*, just in the same way and for the same reason as comic farces and shows were introduced into the religious performances of the Middle Ages. Indeed, the imitation of animals contains in germ the faculty of comic acting, and even nations who have attained a comparatively very low standard, such as the Australians, have surprised Europeans and called forth their admiration by the perfect way in which they mimicked white men. At the Polynesian *Hura*, a kind of family balls, when the young girls were tired of dancing, merry clowns came forward and filled up the pauses with burlesque capers and gesticulations; but the comical intermezzo properly so called, which contains a real action, or at least a dramatic point, and offers an opportunity for genuine mimic art, probably did not exist previously to the historical pantomime. It did not, however, form part of the historical action; its object was to relieve the mind from the impression produced by the seriousness of the play. Sometimes these diversions consisted only of coarse dances or merry love songs, but we also meet with instances of ingenious little scenes which offer good opportunities for artistic and amusing mimic play, as shown in the following scene reported from the Philippine Islands. A wanderer appears who is overcome with fatigue and half starved. All at once he discovers a bee-hive full of honey. Delighted with this lucky discovery, he looks

forward to satisfying his appetite on the delicate fare.
He sets fire to some twigs, and sneaks on tiptoe up to
the hive. First he burns himself, then his throat is
filled with smoke, and at last he is attacked by the bees
who are heard humming all round, while the man fights
about in a ludicrous manner expressive of the pain caused
by their stings.[1]

In the account of Cook's first expedition we are told
how one of the members saw the frequently mentioned
society of Areoi perform a comic pantomime. The
players—all men—were divided into two parties, one of
which wore brown clothes, and represented a man of
rank with his servants; the other party were dressed in
white, and acted as thieves. The master gave his servants a basket with meat, recommending them to take
good care of it. Now the joke was to attempt by every
means to steal the basket from the servants, who did their
best to defend it. All this was done in dancing steps, or
at least in regular rhythmic movements. At last the servants became tired; they sat down in a circle round the
basket. The awakening of the servants, their discovery
of the theft, and their confused searching for the basket,
formed a merry conclusion to this little Tahiti ballet.

The principal *motif* of the scene from the Philippines,
viz., to express mimically and choregraphically the situation of being pursued by a bee, recurs in one of the
favourite pantomimes performed by the *Almahs*:[2] a
young girl is stung by a bee, and dances round, ex-

---

[1] De la Gironière: *Aventures d'un Gentilhomme breton aux Îles philippines*, p. 232.

[2] Almah is the oriental name given to female artists who dance and recite
for the amusement of the ladies of the harem and their protectors.

pressing the pain she feels by her gesticulations, and by her cries of: "Oh, oh, oh, the bee!" Her friends rush up to help her, and in order to find the painful sting they begin by taking off her veil, then her shawl, the next garment and the next, while she continues screaming: "Oh, oh, oh, the bee!" If the spectators' sense of decorum did not interfere in time, she would be undressed to the skin.[1] In the first meeting of Sakuntalâ with King Dushyanta perhaps we find a similar mimic interlude. While the king is hidden among the bushes observing Sakuntalâ and her friends, she discovers a bee flying after her, and in her fright she exclaims: "Ah! a bee, disturbed by the sprinkling of the water, has left the young jasmine, and is trying to settle on my face." (Her movements indicate that she is pursued by a bee.) The king meanwhile looks at her longingly, and says, "Beautiful! there is something charming even in her terror." Then he sings :—

> "Where'er the bee his eager onset plies,
> Now here, now there, she darts her kindling eyes;
> What love has yet to teach, fear teaches now,
> The furtive glances and the frowning brow.
> Ah, happy bee! how boldly dost thou try
> To steal the lustre from her sparkling eye;
> And in thy circling movements hover near,
> To murmur tender secrets in her ear;
> Or, as she coyly waves her hand, to sip
> Voluptuous nectar from her lower lip!
> While rising doubts my heart's fond hopes destroy,
> Thou dost the fulness of her charms enjoy."

We may suppose that while the king was singing his admiration Sakuntalâ performed a kind of dance or

---

[1] Michaud: *Correspondance d'Orient*, v. p. 257.

mimic scene, in which she expressed her childlike and graceful terror of the bee.[1]

Of course many different subjects were used for these comic interludes ; they were generally taken from everyday life, and from a plainer and lower sphere than the historical pantomime, of which in the beginning they formed part. As a rule, however, these little episodes found so great favour with the naïve public that they were soon set apart as independent little dramatic pieces, either pantomimic or in dialogue. Nevertheless, the primitive nations never succeeded in creating either a real comedy or a real tragedy according to our notions. Their imaginative and reflective power was insufficient to create a really connected and finished work of art, and they contented themselves with either playing detached episodes, or linking together and imitating scenes of merely outward reality.

However, before passing on to the history of the European theatre, we have still to examine a few oriental nations whose civilisation was richer and more highly developed than that of primitive peoples, and we shall try to show to what height the theatre and dramatic art were capable of rising among these nations.

[1] Pepita, the Spanish dancer, who in the middle of the last century laid Europe at her feet, is said to have owed her enormous success in a great measure to a dance in which she expressed her fright, and chased—not a bee, but another stinging insect.

THE CHINESE THEATRE

I

THE isolation and mental stagnation of the Chinese has become proverbial. Though the "Great Wall of China," which according to tradition is supposed to enclose the Celestial Empire, does not really exist,[1] it is an appropriate symbol of the prohibition system which has always been a principle in China. The Chinese hates everything foreign, because it is not like his own, because it breaks his traditions and differs from what he and his ancestors do and have always done. This lack of individuality, this uniformity, finds a typical expression in the outward appearance of the Chinese, who, *e.g.*, efface all differences of hair-growth in shaving their heads quite closely, leaving the pigtail as general distinguishing mark of a man ; squeeze the feet of the women to an equal small size, and cover all peculiarities in the structure of the bodies by the same wide garments. It is clear that this repression of all distinctive features cannot be propitious to the development of art, since art derives its principal interest from the individual character that shines through it. Whatever high standard of manual skill art has reached in China, it is probably difficult, even to a Chinese, to distinguish one master from the other. To dramatic art

[1] All that is found is a long piece of wall built to protect the country against the attacks of the Tartars.

and literature in particular this regulation of all feelings and repression of individuality has been specially detrimental.

For this reason Chinese literature does not contain any drama with a sufficiently individual stamp to raise it to our standard of genuine art. A tragic hero according to our ideas, a man whose peculiar gifts and fate raise him above the ordinary level, would only be considered as a maniac or criminal. At the same time we meet now and then pretty deep observations of everyday characters, and amusing, if grotesque, reproductions of comic types.

The first stages of Chinese scenic art are veiled in the darkness of remote antiquity. The statements about the origin of the drama are so contradictory that they mention periods which lie many centuries apart,[1] and so absurd that they attribute the invention of dramatic art to different emperors. Of course we cannot pay any attention to these theories, which are based upon the errors of native critics. Art cannot be "invented" by an emperor, so much we may take for granted ; and though the Chinese drama as we know it, and as it has no doubt been for many centuries, bears anything but a religious or ideal stamp, though it is as earthbound, shallow and realistic as possible—drawing its subjects from sensational criminal causes or from politics—certain circumstances lead us to the conclusion that its origin is connected with religious worship. To each temple of importance, for example, we find even now a stage attached, which generally consists of a

---

[1] Some scholars trace the origin of the Chinese drama to the 18th century B.C., others to the 9th ; others again limit the course of its development to a period of about six hundred years. Cf. Du Méril, *op. cit.* i. p. 143, notes 1 and 2, and Klein, *op. cit.* iii. p. 105.

simple wooden platform in front of the open temple-hall; it is partly covered by a roof of matting, but is open on three sides. At all religious festivals this stage is used for dramatic performances by strolling actors.[1]

This strongly reminds us of European religious plays of the Middle Ages. We may suppose that the drama, as it became secular, was gradually removed from inside the church, though—contrary to European fashion, but in harmony with the conservative tendency in China— it remained in close connection with the institution to which it owes its origin.

Moreover, the sudden interference in everyday events of supernatural beings, who—like the Greek *deus ex machinâ*, though in a strangely matter-of-fact and quite unmystical way—solve the highly complicated plot, seems to point to an earlier close alliance with the worship of higher beings. This supposition is further confirmed by the frequent unwarranted intermixture of music with the theatrical performances.

However, the Chinese drama in its present state is of anything but a mystically religious character ; it is grossly realistic, and drawn in crude, angular lines. Everything is rendered with the highest degree of realism and minuteness, and the spectators would rather outrage all sense of decency than lose a single detail prescribed in the play. When it contains such events as a seduction, a wedding or a birth, they expect to see, and they do see, details of the most private nature represented on the stage. To give an idea of the graphic power and gro-

[1] J. Henningsen : *Det himmelske Rige*, p. 146.

tesqueness which sometimes characterise the dialogue, we quote a little scene from the comedy of " The Miser," an interesting counterpart of the character plays by Plautus and Molière.

The miser lies on his deathbed and gives the last instructions to his son.   He says :

My son, I feel I have not much time left.   Tell me, in what kind of coffin do you mean to bury me?

THE SON.

If I should be unfortunate enough to lose my father, I will buy him the finest deal coffin I can find.

THE MISER.

Don't be so mad! deal is much too expensive. When we are dead we don't see any difference between deal and willow.   Isn't there an old trough behind the house?   That would be quite good enough for a coffin.

THE SON.

What are you thinking of?—That trough is as broad as it is long; it wouldn't fit you, you are too tall.

THE MISER.

Well, if the trough is too short, it is easy enough to shorten my body.   Take an axe and part me in the middle; if you put the two halves on the top of each other, you can get them in easily.   And I have another important thing to say to you.   Don't use my good axe for cutting my body; you may borrow our neighbour's.

THE SON.

As we have got one ourselves, why should we borrow our neighbour's?

THE MISER.

I will tell you why ; my bones are extremely hard, and if you cut them with the edge of my good axe, you will have to spend some pence on getting it sharpened. . . .

The savage coolness of these lines gives a good idea of one side of Chinese art: a tendency to absurd exaggeration, which nevertheless lacks the power of rising to full comic or tragic imagination. But even so distinct a characterisation as we find in the above-quoted example is quite exceptional. As a rule the persons of the play are only distinguished from each other by their names and by certain circumstances of their lives, which they make haste to state as soon as they appear on the stage. Thus for instance : " I live in Tung-ping-fu, my surname is Lihu, my name Tsung-sjang. I am sixty years old, and Li-sji, my wife, is fifty-eight." Or : " Hang-kué is a warrior, equally noted for his magnanimity and for his valour." [1]

We find this simple method of enlightening the spectators also in European plays, especially in those of the Middle Ages ; nor does Scribe, otherwise celebrated for his skilful technique, despise this primitive proceeding, though he knows how to hide it in various more or less ingenious ways. The whole construction of the

[1] Ed. du Méril, *La Comédie ancienne*, pp. 147 ff.

Chinese play is on a level with it, and shows that the development of the drama must have stopped long, long ago. The scene changes in a moment from heaven to hell and back to the earth ; gods and animals are mixed up with the action in the most uncalled-for way, just as in nursery tales (fig. 8). These fantastic interventions are probably due to ancient traditions, which the Chinese have been as unwilling to give up as all other traditional customs. Probability of time is no more consulted than probability of place, and so little trouble is taken to hide these absurdities that they appear utterly ridiculous to an eye accustomed to modern stage technique. Thus in a play called " The Songstress," a traveller asks his landlord to send for some singers. The landlord answers : " It shall be done," and instantly adds : " I may inform your honour that the singers have arrived."[1]

For the rest, incongruities of this kind occur everywhere in the primitive stages of the drama. In the "Antigone " of Sophocles, for instance, Creon orders a guard to call the man who has buried the body of Polynices ; the guard goes and comes back two minutes after, reporting events which have taken place in the meantime, but which in real life would have taken at least half a day. After all, we are no doubt too ready to carp at Chinese oddities, without bearing sufficiently in mind that the European theatre possesses similar absurdities, though they may appear under a slightly different form. Indeed, scenic art rests to a very great extent on convention, and

---

[1] Quoted by Ed. du Méril, *La Comédie ancienne*, vol. i.

what we think ludicrous and grotesque may very often be due only to conventional differences.

There is one absurd custom which we meet with in Chinese as well as in European plays, viz., the frequent intermixture of song with the dialogue whenever deeper feelings are to be expressed. For instance, in an author like Hostrup,[1] it has never struck a modern public how ludicrous it is to hear the actors express their feelings in song where they become pathetic, while all critics agree in laughing at the same proceeding when it occurs in Chinese plays. As an example we quote one of the most celebrated plays, which may also serve as a sample of the serious Chinese dramatic style. Its title is, *The Chalk Circle*.[2] The subject of this drama is a criminal cause : a lawsuit between two women, both of whom pretend to be the mother of the same child. A rich Chinese of high rank, named Ma, has married a courtesan besides his legitimate wife. The name of this woman is Haï-Thang, and he loves her far more than his lawful wife, who in no way deserves his love. The wife on her side has a lover, with whom she agrees to poison her husband, so that they may enjoy his wealth in peace. In a dish which she orders the concubine to prepare and to serve for her husband (intending to accuse her of the murder afterwards), she mixes a poisonous powder, with which her lover has provided her. The husband dies immediately after eating it, and Haï-Thang is accused of the crime.

---

[1] A modern Danish dramatist.
[2] *Hoei-lan-ki*, translated by Stanislas Lucien under the title of *L'histoire du Cercle de Craie*, London, 1832.

But this is not all ; Haï-Thang has borne a son to Ma, and this child is his rightful heir. Now the legitimate wife bribes the servants to swear that it is her own child.

If this stratagem succeeds, Ma's fortune will fall into the hands of the wife and her lover. The affair is brought to the law courts ; and after the unfortunate Haï-Thang has gone through all manner of mental and physical torture, the cause is put before the wise supreme judge Pao-Tsching. He orders a circle to be drawn on the floor of the hall of justice, and inside this circle the child is placed. The Chinese Solomon pronounces the sentence that both women are to pull the child, each from one side, and that she who succeeds in drawing it outside the circle is the real mother. They obey, and the false mother at once pulls the child towards herself, while the real mother stands alone, disgraced. Thereupon the wise judge calls the executioner and orders him to whip the innocent Haï-Thang. However, she stops him and proves her innocence and her right by a monologue which is the *clou* of the piece. She says :—

"I beseech thee, master, tame thy wrath, which frightens me more than the rolling thunder, and soften thy threatening glance, which is awful as that of the wolf and the tiger. When thy humble servant was married to the honourable lord Ma, she gave birth shortly afterwards to this little child. After having borne it under my heart for nine months, I nourished it three years with my own milk, and I nursed it with all the care which motherly love prescribes. When it felt cold I warmed its tiny limbs. Oh, what pains I took to rear it till it was five years old! Weak and fragile as it is, it could not be pulled from both sides without being seriously hurt. If I cannot get back my son without breaking his arms and legs, I would rather be beaten to death than make the slightest effort to get him out of the circle. I hope your honour will have pity on me. (*She sings.*) How could a tender mother bring her heart to do this? (*She speaks.*) Master, look here for thyself! (*She sings.*) The arms of this child are soft and brittle like the stem of flax when the bark is peeled off. Should this hard inhuman woman be able to understand my fear? And thou, master, how canst thou help discovering the truth? Ah! how different are our positions! She has influence and money, I am despised and humiliated. Indeed, if we both pulled this tiny child violently, thou would'st hear its bones crack, thou would'st see its flesh fall off in tatters."

And Pao-Tsching, the wise judge, who—after the fashion of judges in the world of poetry—has known the truth all the time, solves the highly strung plot with the following knotty speech: "Though the sense of the law is hard to understand, it is possible, nevertheless, to find out the thoughts of the human heart. An old sage has pronounced these deep words: 'What man would be able to hide his own character, if once you had observed his actions, tried the motive of his work, and recognised the goal he had placed before himself? Look what an awful power lies in this circle of chalk! In her innermost heart this woman (Ma's wife) wished

to usurp all her husband's wealth, therefore she wanted
to possess herself of the child.   But sooner or later the
truth will come to light!"

II

The Theatre — Its Unofficial Character — Chinese Social Comedy — The
Public and its Attitude—Construction of the Stage — Equipment
and Costumes — Actors — The Pupils of the Imperial "Pear-
garden"—Professional Training of the Actors—Salary and Social
Position.

In the theatre where these plays are enacted, no
attempts are made to call forth illusion or to produce
on the feelings, by decorations, lighting, etc., those
effects which form an essential part of the pleasure of
European playgoers.   Whether from well - meditated
principle, or—which is more likely—from faithfulness
to old custom, the only means of effect are words and
movements.   The stage, in fact, is nothing but a platform on which the actors play without any support but
their personality and talent, and the public does not seem
to miss the scenic apparatus, which has become indispensable to us ; it is left to fancy to imagine the necessary
decorations.   At first, in China as in all other countries,
plays were only acted at festivals and on solemn occasions, not by professional actors, but by amateurs, and
not in a special building set apart for the purpose, but on
a platform erected for the occasion, consisting simply of a
wooden floor supported by trestles ; and the Chinese stage
has, to a certain extent, retained this incidental character.

Not even at the present day do we find *public* buildings for regular theatrical performances ; even private
play-houses are of quite exceptional occurrence, and only
found in towns of considerable size.   The fact that the
Government keeps aloof from all theatrical matters has
been taken as a proof that dramatic art is illegal, and only
tolerated ; moreover, that it is a pleasure for the lower
classes only, and inconsistent both with the ideas of the
cultivated Chinaman and with all national traditions.
This view, however, is quite mistaken.   No Chinese law
forbids acting, and plays are a favourite entertainment of
the people.   Everywhere, at national and religious festivals, at weddings, fairs, private parties and in the larger
taverns, dramatic performances are the chief part of the
entertainment, and seem to have been so for centuries.
The emperor himself does not disdain to appear as an
actor.   Playing in private houses seems to have always
formed an important part of the professional actor's
work, and is still considered one of the principal sources
of his income.   In a book of travels of the middle of the
seventeenth century we find a rather curious description
of tavern plays, which in the main applies to the
present state of affairs.   The account runs thus : "One
of the things in China which may well surprise us is the
fact that each hostelry or inn has its own company of
actors, just as in our own country every village inn is wont
to have its fiddler during fair-time.   These comedians,
in order to amuse the guests, act during the meals all
kinds of merry, amusing and burlesque plays, and all of
them—men and women—are richly adorned with various
magnificent garments and trappings.   They are always

prepared to perform several of the generally familiar plays, so that at the request of the guests they may act any of them at once.   They also show the guests a book in which all their plays are written in the Chinese language, so that they may choose one of them, which they would like to see.   But these plays are nearly always adapted for singing, scarcely ever for ordinary speech.   For a repast, including drink and play, we did not pay more than two *mans* (nowadays about one shilling), not much of which could fall to the share of the actors.   Therefore we wondered much whence these people got the money which they had to spend on fine clothes and other necessaries, as their performances are so badly paid." [1]

Of theatricals in private houses a modern traveller [2] gives a similar description : "As soon as the guests have sat down to dinner, four or five richly dressed actors enter the hall ; they bow so respectfully and so nimbly that they touch the floor four times with their foreheads. Then one of them presents to the highest in rank of the persons present a book in which the titles of from fifty to sixty plays are written in golden letters.   These plays they know by heart, and can act on the spur of the moment.   The most distinguished guest chooses the piece, and the performance begins with beating drums of buffalo - skin and playing on flutes, shalms and trumpets.   The space between the two rows of tables is used as a stage.   A carpet is spread on the floor, and

---

[1] Neuhof : *Gesandschaft der ostindischen Gesellschaft in den vereinigten Niederlanden.*   Amsterdam, 1669, quoted by Klein, iii. p. 408.

[2] E. F. Timkowsky : *Travels of the Russian Mission*, translated by H. E. Lloyd.   London, 1827.

for want of 'wings' the actors use the adjoining rooms, from which they come out when they are going to act. They always play by daylight."

Though, of course, the regular theatres exhibit more apparatus, we do not find that great trouble is taken to arrest the attention of the spectators, and the plays bear the same character as those previously described, being a light, pleasant entertainment, which the spectators enjoy with their meals. Though it is forbidden by law to act after sunset, the theatres now allow their regular performances to go on till late at night. They generally begin at five or six in the afternoon; but, as four or five long pieces are often acted consecutively, they seldom finish till after midnight, and the authorities wink at this transgression of a law which has long fallen into disuse. Together with his ticket the spectator receives a programme printed on scarlet paper, a cup of tea and a pipe. The play-hall, as a rule, is pretty large, and well lighted by coloured paper lanterns. The best places are in the middle of the floor, and here the persons of high rank are seated at small tables, on which the tea is steaming out of dainty china cups. The ladies sparkle in their gold-embroidered dresses; their glossy black hair is built up artificially with a whole flower-basket rocking on its top, and their long nails shine in pink enamel edged with blue or green, vying in gaudiness with their brightly painted faces. The gentlemen suck their small pipes with dignity, enjoying the wonders on the stage with naïve admiration. But in the low upper gallery, which runs along three sides of the hall, the lower-class public amuses itself noisily by talking, laughing, eating and drinking, going in and out without much regard to the play. And, indeed, if the spectators do not want to pledge themselves to silence the whole evening, they must talk during the performance, for there are no pauses between the acts or the pieces. The titles of the plays and the names of the actors are written in the programme, but if a spectator is not satisfied with the play announced, he may choose another, and for a comparatively small payment have it performed at a moment's notice, as soon as one of the actors has informed the public of the change.

The stage consists of a platform four or five feet high, at the back of the hall. It is framed with red drapery, and at the sides are closed boxes for spectators. A front curtain is unknown, nor are there "wings" or any other decorations. The background is a canvas partition which, according to very ancient custom, has two doors, one serving only as entrance, the other only as exit.[1] A few pieces require—contrary to the oldest custom—a third door, the "ghost entrance," *Kvei-men*, through which only supernatural beings are allowed to pass.

The orchestra is placed in sight of the public between the doors on the stage ; it is composed of flute and clarinet players, but its chief ingredient is drummers and kettle-drummers. It is the chief task of this orchestra, whenever a sentence calls for particular attention, to

[1] To "enter" on the stage is expressed in Chinese by the word *sjang* (= he mounts), the word "exit" by *hia* (= he descends), because in the original open-air theatres the stage was so narrow that the actors had to climb up and down to get in and out of the doors.

underline it with a deafening accompaniment on their noisy instruments.

The stage is furnished with a table and a couple of chairs, which always remain, whatever place the stage is supposed to represent. That no decorative apparatus is used in plays which would require constant and very difficult scene-shiftings, if our standard of illusion were to be satisfied, is neither unreasonable nor ridiculous, especially if we consider that these plays are frequently performed in private houses, which naturally precludes all scenic arrangements. The slight attempts which are nevertheless made by Chinese stage managers to guide the imagination of the public cannot fail to strike European eyes on account of their extreme *naïveté*.

A wood, for instance, is represented by tying a green branch to a chair-back. The apparently difficult problem of conducting an army to some remote province is solved in the following very simple and unmistakable way : the leader takes a whip in one hand and a bridle in the other, and gallops round the stage accompanied by loud music from the band ; at last he informs the spectators that he has arrived at his destination. The passing from one room into another is expressed by making a movement which indicates the opening of a door, and lifting a leg as if crossing a threshold. A wall surrounding a town is represented either by a piece of calico held up by two coolies, or, in a more decorative but less comprehensible fashion, by three or four supers lying down one on the top of another in a corner of the stage.

In contrast with this perfect indifference to stage equipment stands the care which the actor must devote to his artistic training as well as to his outward appearance in each special part. If the Chinese spectator shows great forbearance with regard to the naïve improbabilities of the *mise-en-scène*, he is very exacting in his demands for accuracy of costume and the correct masking of traditional figures, — " masking " here used for what modern European theatre-language calls "make-up." In China real masks are only used in pantomimes for special grossly exaggerated villains. As will be seen from the above-quoted remarks by Neuhof, even strollers and tavern companies consider it necessary to appear in very expensive costumes, and in theatres of any distinction it is imperative, not only that the dresses should be rich, but above all that they should be minute copies of the old traditional patterns (fig. 9).

As above stated, great pains are taken with the professional—though probably merely outward—training of the actors. As a class they go by the strange name of " Pupils of the Imperial Pear-garden," an expression which dates from the eighteenth century of our era, when the emperor Tang-Ming-Huang established the first school of scenic art and music. The emperor himself trained a hundred young singing girls, and his instruction was given in an orchard belonging to the imperial palace.

Originally, no doubt, women appeared on the stage ; even now there are towns where the female parts are acted by women, nor is there any law which forbids them to act in public performances. But women are not allowed to play at court festivals, and the reason of this law is that an emperor of the present dynasty took

8

9

8—Scene from a Chinese play.   9—Chinese actors.

an actress as concubine and had a son by her, named Kien-Lung, who afterwards gained fame by his liberality and his learning. On his accession he humoured his mother by forbidding women to act at court, probably in order to spare her from being reminded too directly of her earlier profession.

Nowadays the female parts are generally represented by men, and public feeling forbids women to appear as actresses. It may be that this sense of decorum arose only as an after-effect of court etiquette, but it may be also that the gross erotic scenes which, as we have said, are not uncommon in Chinese plays, found a kind of excuse in the fact that they were only performed by men. The training of the men who are intended for female parts begins at a very early age. A manager buys the children, and in the school of art particular care is taken to develop their falsetto and their memory. That this training is not carried out by the gentlest means, we see from contracts between parents and theatrical managers, which frequently contain clauses to the effect that the former cannot claim compensation in case the stage-training of their children should lead to their being whipped to death. On the other hand, the result obtained, in the case of those who escape alive from this school, is so perfect, that it is said to be almost impossible to distinguish one of these male actresses from a real woman (fig. 10).

All actors, indeed, receive a systematic education, which as a rule lasts three or four years. Each pupil is taught one special branch, and he neither wishes nor is allowed to act in any other. It is natural enough that one

who impersonates women cannot study male parts as
well, considering the way in which his voice is trained;
but it is equally out of the question to make a hero play
a villain, or the latter a comic part. A similar division,
we know, exists in Europe; in Germany especially, an
actor will frequently seek engagement as "first lover"
or as character player, and the parts which, according to
tradition, belong to these categories invariably fall to
his share, without considering whether or not they suit
his nature. Fortunately, however, this mechanical and
spiritless conception of the means of effect in dramatic
art seems to be gradually falling into disuse.

In China the limitation of each actor to one special
branch is no doubt due in a great measure to the different
training of the voices, but it is also necessitated by
another circumstance: the pupils of the imperial "pear-
garden" as a rule are unable to read, so they can only
learn their parts through the ear, and it is clear that the
manager, who has the task of literally whipping the
sentences into their memories, prefers to give each of
his pupils as homogeneous tasks as possible. The
average stock of each actor consists of from fifty to
sixty plays, and he must have all his parts at his fingers'
ends, for the office of prompter is unknown in China,
and the actor must be ready at any moment to perform
the part required by the manager or the public.

As to the specification and number of the different
branches, the reports are very contradictory: some
authors mention eleven, others four or three; and they
are not clearly defined. By comparing the most trustworthy statements, it seems to me that the parts may

be divided into two principal groups, the male and the female, each being subdivided into four sections.

Male parts : (1) *the old man* (emperor, head of the family, statesman, etc. ; in European theatres, *père noble*) ; (2) *the young man* (hero, lover, dandy ; in Europe, hero and lover parts) ; (3) *the villain*, called the "painted face" (in Europe, character-actor or villain) ; (4) *the comic actor*, whose parts belong mainly to two subdivisions : the obscene comic parts and *tsjéu*, the ludicrous monsters.

The four female sections are : (1) the *old woman* (*lao-tan*) ; (2) the *first female lover* (*tsjing-tan* : primadonna) ; (3) the *young girl* (*siao-tan*) ; and (4) the *slave girl* (whose nearest European equivalent is the soubrette).[1]

We cannot guarantee the absolute correctness of this classification, but it seems to be the most reasonable conclusion that can be drawn from the various divergent statements.

The salary of the actor varies according to his line of parts. The hero is best paid ; he may rise as high as about £500 a year. The comic actor is the least esteemed and gets the lowest remuneration. However, acting in private houses adds considerably to his income.

In spite of the extreme pleasure which the Chinese undoubtedly find in theatrical performances, dramatic literature and scenic art enjoy but very slight consideration in

---

[1] Comp. among others, Ed. du Méril : *op. cit.* i. p. 150, and notes i. to xi. Henningsen : *Det himmelske Rige*, p. 148. Klein : *Geschichte des Dramas*, iii. p. 411.

China, and the actors as a class occupy a very low rank. The theatre is no established institution, and there is a law which forbids the sons of actors, barbers and slaves to enter for public examinations, thus excluding these unfortunates from every chance of rising above their position and of occupying State offices ; and the shame of belonging to the despised class of actors casts its shadow over many subsequent generations.   According to an old statute, actresses were placed on a par with prostitutes, and the word *tan*—still used for female parts—originally meant "*a lustful animal.*"   That this contempt reacts on the players and leads them to be contemptible persons is a natural consequence, and a fact frequently experienced in other cases.   What applies to their persons may also be said of their art. However fond the Chinese public may be of the theatre, they do not look to it for refined or intellectual influences. And they get what they want—a light recreation, nothing more.

Therefore, scenic art in China continues to be what it always was : a systematic, carefully prepared *amusement*, perfect of its kind, but wanting in individual character and the intellectual stamp which ought to raise it to the level of real art (fig. 11).

10

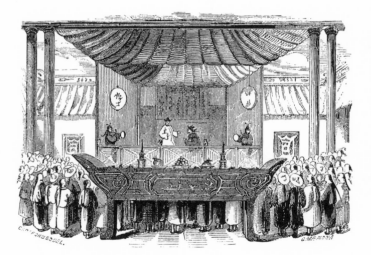

11

10—Chinese actor in female costume.   11—Chinese theatre.

THE JAPANESE THEATRE

Legends of its Origin—Street and Procession Plays in Ancient Times—
Children as Actors—The Modern Japanese Theatre—Course of the
Performances—Auditorium and Stage—Peculiar Arrangement—The
Actors and their Method of Playing.

LEGEND tells us that in the ninth century a violent earth-
quake took place in Japan, in the province of Yamato ;
poisonous vapours emanated from the deep, spreading
death and destruction all round. Nothing could overcome
the awful scourge, until the priests conceived the idea of
performing a symbolic dance of incantation on a grass-
covered hill outside the temple. At once the pestiferous
vapour vanished, and peace and happiness were restored
to the country. And the legend adds that this was
indeed how Japanese acting originated. *Shibai-ya*, the
Japanese word for theatre, reminds us of this supposed
origin, as *shibai* means " sod " and *ya* " a house." Even
nowadays the great miracle of Yamato is celebrated by
the same religious dance as an introduction to every
performance. Just as in India every drama begins with
a prayer, in Japan an actor dressed like an old priest
appears at the commencement of each play, swings his
fan and performs a rhythmic dance, while a chorus
implores the mercy of the saving divinities in plaintive
and mystic songs.[1]

Though, of course, neither this legend nor any others
which attribute the birth of dramatic art to a single

[1] George Bousquet : *Le théâtre au Japon* (*Revue des deux Mondes*,
1874), vol. iv. p. 729.

mythical event have any historical value, since the nature
of art precludes its being thus invented, the Japanese
tradition is interesting in so far as it shows that here,
as everywhere, the drama was originally connected
with religious cult.

The development through which the national theatre
in Japan has passed from its ritual origin shows in many
ways a striking resemblance to our mediæval forms of
scenic art. The Japanese drama has been somewhat
neglected by the historians of dramatic literature ; they
either pass it over in silence, or treat it with a carelessness which reveals their lack of interest in the subject.
Nevertheless, scattered reports by travellers and a few
independent essays, which form the only material for
investigation, offer certain starting-points which seem to
deserve attention, partly on account of their originality,
partly because of their striking resemblance to the
theatrical records of the European Middle Ages.

On certain feast days stages are built outside the
larger temples ; they consist of a wooden platform about
six feet above the ground, and are covered by a roof, with
the four upward-turned corners characteristic of the monuments of ancient Japan. This roof rests, like a canopy,
on slender pillars, so that the stage is open on three
sides, while the fourth, which abuts on the front of the
temple, is closed. On this stage, bizarre pantomimes are
acted, in which the religious element is mingled with the
coarsest jokes. These plays are performed by boys, who
in many cases are only from ten to twelve years old, and
European spectators have admired the extreme coolness
with which these youngsters acted the mimic parts and

delivered the dialogues. Their dresses are magnificent, and they wear masks which are painted with the sense for gross exaggeration which is one of the chief talents of the Japanese. The masks, which are only used in dances or pantomimes, are held with the teeth by a small wooden plate fixed inside, similar to those we see among some savage nations. While on other occasions the temples, as a rule, are pretty empty, huge crowds are attracted by these spectacles, which are the more popular because they are gratuitous, being paid for either by the State or by the priests.

Though these temple-plays bear so close a resemblance to those in China, it may be doubted whether they are due to the influence of Chinese civilisation. Their likeness to European mediæval " mysteries " is nearly as striking, and as far as the latter are concerned, we may say for certain that no influence can have been exercised. These remarkable similarities recur constantly in the history of dramatic art, as well as in the general civilisation of mankind ; but we must no doubt be careful not to conclude anything from this circumstance but that the human mind at equal stages of civilisation always seems to work under the same laws, and therefore produces results which, even in widely different nations, are surprisingly alike.

A modern traveller tells us that one night, when passing through a well-known sacred village about twenty miles from Yeddo, he suddenly heard from the depths of a fir-wood some strange music, which seemed quite inexplicable at so late an hour of the night. He followed the sound and saw disguised figures moving about in the wood, dancing in the torchlight and singing peculiar monotonous songs. He found out that they were celebrating a festival in honour of Fudo-sama. However, if the French author to whom we owe this description thinks that the young village actors chose this hour for the same reason which made him travel at night, viz., on account of its comparative coolness—the thing happened in August—he is no doubt mistaken. This nightly festival is evidently a survival from an earlier stage of civilisation, when the Japanese honoured their gods by performing mystic dances by moonlight or torchlight, like the Australians, the American Indians, and other savage nations.

We see another somewhat more advanced stage in the peculiar *street performances* connected with processions, which still exist as a popular amusement, and which are analogous to the mediæval street "mysteries," especially seen in England. It is always a religious festival which occasions the street plays and processions, and it is the congregation which defrays the expenses ; each street equips its procession and provides for the training of its actors. As a rule, however, these plays are performed by children, in former times probably by boys and girls, at present no doubt exclusively by boys. The subjects of these pieces are mythological and heroic, but mingled with comic scenes which have nothing to do with the action of the play, just as in the European "mysteries." A great part of these comedies is acted in dumb show.

The above-quoted Engelbrecht Kämpfer gives a graphic account of the processional plays as they were performed in his time, the seventeenth century. He describes a festival which celebrated the birth of the god Suwa.[1]

"The street," he says, "at the expense of which the entertainment is given, arranges the procession in the following order :—First comes the palladium of the street, a costly sunshade, in the middle of which the name of the street is written. Close behind follow the musicians with flutes and drums ; their music is miserable ; though it may please the gods, it cannot possibly be agreeable to human ears. . . . It must be confessed that they show much cleverness and ingenuity in their dances ; in this point they are scarcely inferior to Europeans. Next to the musicians come those who bear the necessary appliances for the performance and the decoration of the stage, the heavier objects being carried by artisans, the lighter ones, such as chairs, staves, flowers, etc., by the children from the street which pays for the entertainment, all in brilliant dresses. Finally the actors, followed by all the inhabitants of the street in their festive attire. . . . The street-dancing lasts for about three-quarters of an hour, after which the procession marches on to other streets, which add their share of followers to the troop. The streets vie with each other in getting up these entertainments as magnificently as possible. They begin quite early in the morning and end about noon. . . . Each year there must be new properties and different spectacles and dances ; it would be thought beneath the dignity of

[1] Suwa is the Indian god Siva, whom some of the Greeks considered identical with Dionysus (Dewasiva). According to this opinion, the Suwa festivals would be the Dionysia of the Japanese. Comp. Klein, *op. cit.* p. 507.

the patron if anything from the preceding year were reproduced. . . ."

We are unable to throw much light on Japanese theatrical matters on account of the scantiness and poverty of available sources; and the scattered notes offered here only concern the *national* theatre. The Japanese, who are of a receptive nature, with a marked tendency to imitation of all foreign things and customs, soon came strongly under the influence of Chinese civilisation, and this influence was very marked with regard to the stage. A kind of Chinese drama was created, while the national drama remained in its primitive, half-pantomimic state, just as in Europe the national scenic art of the Middle Ages was stopped in its growth by the direct imitation of classical literature introduced by the Renaissance. It is not unlikely that the Japanese theatre of the present day will receive a similar influence from Europe, and that ere long we shall see French matrimonial dramas acted in coats of some sort and tall hats by the small inhabitants of the "sun-land," and therewith the loss of every characteristic of the national scenic art. But at present these characteristics still exist; they are even so marked, and so different from anything known in any other nation, that they deserve some attention.

Whereas the drama and the art of acting have kept pretty close to the Chinese types, the construction of the stage has undergone great alterations. The Japanese, with their bright and restless imagination, could not long be contented with the simple, uninteresting frame, within which their emotional and graphic plays were represented, and which for centuries had satisfied the conservative Chinese. So they created a stage which corresponded better with the character of their dramas, and a few of these reforms are indeed so ingenious that it would be worth while to consider whether they might not be of use to European theatres.

The hours of these spectacles also differ from the Chinese; they begin at six o'clock in the morning. At sunrise the drums are beaten outside the play-house, and crowds rush to the office to buy tickets. This early hour —so extraordinary to us—causes a great deal of inconvenience to the Japanese, too, but they are so fond of this amusement that they willingly get up in order to enjoy it from the beginning. It is not considered proper for men of rank, high officials or learned men to be present at the performance of a play, but their ladies do not deny themselves the pleasure of going *incognito* to enjoy this popular art, though in Japan, as well as in China, it is looked upon as anything but a noble or even respectable profession. The early hours are even more inconvenient to ladies than to gentlemen, as their elaborate toilette must be commenced on the previous night. The hairdresser has to come the day before and build up the artificial structure which is the pride of every Japanese lady. This of course obliges her to spend the night in her state dress, reclining her head on a kind of block called *makura*.[1] Truly a self-sacrifice on the part of the spectators which European actors might envy their oriental brethren! The painting of neck, breast and face may be put off till

[1] G. Bousquet : *Le Théâtre au Japon.*

the morning if the lady rises very early, but she must not forget to cover her lips with the thin layer of gold used by the Japanese as lip-paint, as it takes several hours for this paint to change into the cherry colour which lends charm to the artificial white complexion of the face.   In compensation for all this trouble the Japanese lady is not put off with a European three hours' play.   As a rule the performance lasts from 6 A.M. to 9 P.M., and certain historical dramas, which—in Japan as in China—follow the life of the hero through all its vicissitudes till his death, may even go on for several days.

The Japanese theatres—contrary to the rule with other buildings—are distinguished by their great height; they are, moreover, easily recognised by the peculiar projecting structure on their roofs, in which—as in a kind of main-top—a look-out-man is placed, whose business it is to give warning in case of fire.   In front, the building is covered with cloth posters bearing full-size pictures of the most important scenes of the play which is being acted. Each entrance—as a rule there are only two—is guarded by a seller of tickets, who sits on the ground surrounded by high piles of small coin.   The play-hall is a large square room, the far part forming the stage, which —unlike Chinese, but similar to European fashion— is separated from the other part of the hall by a cloth curtain.   The auditorium is divided into a number of square boxes of equal size, separated by low partitions. Each of them has room for four persons placed opposite to each other and sideways to the stage.   Between them stands a warming-pan with embers, at which the gentlemen keep lighting their copper pipes.   The

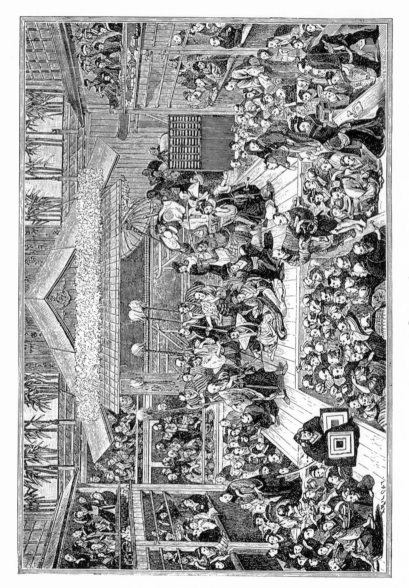

12—Japanese theatre.

other necessaries of life, indispensable at such long entertainments, are served on the broad tops of the partitions between the boxes, which occupy the whole floor. A balcony runs along the upper part of the walls; its front boxes contain the best seats, which are especially coveted by the upper classes. The floor is occupied by the middle classes, and the amphitheatre behind the balcony by the lowest and poorest people. In the middle of the hall an inspector is stationed on a platform and has to keep an eye on the whole theatre and see that order is maintained. To the left of the spectators a projecting box close to the stage contains the orchestra and a band of singers; the musical instruments are drums, flutes and the characteristic three-stringed guitar, *samsin*. The musicians wear magnificent dresses—a survival from the religious origin of the theatre. Good-sized Japanese auditoriums have room for fifteen hundred persons (fig. 12).

As one of the peculiar characteristics of the Japanese stage we may mention two parallel passages which traverse the whole length of the auditorium and lead up to the background of the hall. These passages are on a level with the boxes on the floor, and are used by the actors for going up to the stage; sometimes they will linger on the way and spend as long as ten minutes in expressing their feelings by pantomimic play. Of course these passages have no decorations at all. Contrary to Chinese custom, the Japanese theatre is comparatively very advanced in its scenic painting, and accessories and requisites are executed with an exceedingly realistic accuracy. But the most astonishing achievement is the Japanese method of scene-shifting.

Both the Japanese and the Chinese historical drama require a multitude of changes, but while the Chinese—like the Shaksperian—drama disdains all decorative art, the Japanese, centuries ago, found out an easy and ingenious way of frequent scene-shifting. On a previous page, where the Japanese pantomime is mentioned, we quoted a sentence from an old book of travels in Japan, and promised an explanation of the following words: "The principal accessories of the stage, such as wells, bridges, gates, houses, gardens, mountains or animals, are represented as naturally as possible, *and are so contrived that, just as on the European stage, they can instantly be removed or taken to pieces at a given signal.*" Evidently the learned traveller did not understand how these changes were effected, or he would scarcely have omitted to describe the proceeding; at any rate he would not have compared it with European scene-shifting. The thing is done in this way: the floor of the stage in its whole length and width consists of a circular plate, which can be turned round like the disks on which our railway-engines are shunted. This plate is divided by the back-cloth into two halves, only one of which is visible to the public at a time. At a given signal the scene is shifted by turning the plate with all that is on it. The actors continue talking till they are out of sight, and the other half comes round and faces the public. Owing to this simple contrivance, the Japanese need not recoil from any changes of scene, and they make such ample use of it, that half a score of turnings may be counted in an hour.

While this invention might seem practical enough to be used even in well-developed European machinery,[1] we meet with another peculiar arrangement, which is quite incompatible with our ideas of illusion. It is the living machine which Bousquet calls the *shadow*. Each actor on the boards is followed by a disguised figure dressed in black and with a black hood on its head. The only business of this strange apparition is to wait upon the actor by handing to him the objects he wants, placing chairs, lighting up his face when the stage is dark, etc. Though at first it is irritating to the foreign spectator to see this black figure constantly wandering about the stage, it is said that the eye can get accustomed to it, and at last find it indispensable.

Officially the social position of actors is not better in Japan than in China ; they belong to the lowest classes of society. But in reality they enjoy much more consideration and are idolised by the general public. A few of them have even been mourned by the whole people after their death, and buried with great pomp at the public expense. As a rule, their salaries are but small, not amounting to much more than one thousand *rios* (about £220), but the leading actors are generally part-owners of the theatre, and in this capacity gain the greater part of their income.

In Japan, as in China, women are not allowed to

---

[1] Quite recently—in 1896—Lautenschläger, the well-known master of the scenery of the Munich Court Theatre, has introduced a very similar apparatus for scene-shifting, which is used, for instance, in Mozart's *Don Giovanni*.

appear on the boards, but the education of men for the female parts seems to be very inferior to the Chinese as far as voice-training goes.   Though in appearance and movements they can imitate the other sex to the life, they have great trouble in disguising their voices under the shrill snuffling speech which has become traditional.

Otherwise (as we have said) Japanese scenic art does not differ essentially from the Chinese.   It shows a great tendency to purely mechanical imitation of indifferent realistic details, and at the same time to grossly exaggerated passion in its most palpable forms.   Violent paroxysms of fury and vengeance, crude pathological imitations of the horrors of agony, seem to be the special attainments of the Japanese actor, by which he reaps his greatest fame.   Nor does he spare himself in performing these tasks.   The worst European ranter is a mere log compared with the Japanese hero when he gets into a passion.   His diction flies up and down in the most violent contrasts, now shaking the walls with sonorous voice, now wheezing almost inaudibly, all in a uniform rhythmic chanting declamation which does not in the least resemble human speech.   Sometimes he can find no words, and stops altogether, expressing the climax of his fury only through pantomimic action.   It is in these scenes that the Japanese actor attains the perfection of pantomimic art : he foams, grinds his teeth, rolls his eyes, tears great tufts of hair out of his head, rolls on the floor in terrible convulsions, and dies, amid the cheers of the public, a slow death, of which the audience is not spared a single rattle or the faintest sigh.

A French traveller who had been present at the

performance of a sensational piece of this kind, asked the famous Japanese actor, Sodjuro, why he exaggerated the efforts of his voice and the violence of his gestures to such a degree. " It does not seem to me that a *daïmio* or warrior speaks like that," he added. " No," the actor replied; "but if we behaved on the stage as people do in ordinary life, *who could see that we were heroes?*"

This remark indeed expresses the essence of the Japanese people's conception of art: its ideal representation of man consists in a sharply drawn exaggeration.

THE INDIAN THEATRE

I

ABOUT a hundred years ago appeared the first European translations of Kâlidâsa's play *Sakuntalâ*, the English version by Sir William Jones in 1789, and the German by Georg Forster in 1791. A few years later this play was known to all educated people as one of the masterpieces of literature. Herder published letters about it and wrote his introduction to the German translation, and Goethe composed his famous verse :—

> "Would'st thou the flowers of spring and the fruits of autumn,
> Would'st thou what tempts and charms, what fills and nourishes,
> Would'st thou heaven and earth expressed in one name,
> I mention thee, Sakuntalâ, and all is said."

The overflowing enthusiasm revealed in these lines was hardly without influence on the German Sakuntalâ worship, which found expression in numberless translations, essays, stage-adaptations and musical arrangements. This beautiful love-drama was even represented in Vienna as a ballet a few years ago.

But in Sakuntalâ "all is not said," though Indology made a great start through the general attention called forth by this, the first translated Indian drama. Throughout our century it continued to bring to light a hitherto unknown extensive and important literature which embraces nearly all branches of intellectual life, and is interesting enough to bear comparison with the ancient and mediæval productions of Europe.

However, a science which, like Indology, is but little more than one hundred years old, can only just be said to have emerged from its childhood ; and in spite of the enormous work that has been done, and the many distinguished names already attached to this young science, much is still uncertain or quite in the dark.

This is the case particularly with regard to chronology, not least with the chronology of dramatic literature. It seems scarcely possible that we can possess so little knowledge about Kâlidâsa—who was as famous in his own country as he is in Europe—as to assign his date, now to the first century B.C., now to the eleventh A.D., without more certainty as to either of these hypotheses than allows us, until further notice, to say at present, that he lived in the fifth or sixth century of our era. We explain this ignorance by the remarkable fact that India —though very advanced in other branches of science— possesses no historical science whatever. The Hindoos were a people of philosophers. As to the past, they never questioned "*when?*" but "*how?*" The enigma of creation was the only historical problem that interested them, and as to the future, it was the problem of future existence ; no events, either past or present, appeared worthy of note, since eternal unalterable rest was the common goal of all aspirations.

Therefore we easily understand the great trouble European Indologists have had to get to the bottom of historical questions. If we look at the drama, however, the final result seems to be that its flourishing

period lies between the fifth and the eighth centuries
A.D., that is, between the poets Kâlidâsa and Bhavabhûti.
After the eighth century we still meet with pieces of
interest, before the fifth century with none whatever.
With Kâlidâsa [1] we are introduced into the heart of a
classical literature, the origin and development of which
are quite unknown to us.

Of course there are plenty of legends which attribute
the origin of dramatic art to a divine source. The
Indians themselves suppose its inventor to have been
a mythical person, *Bharata*, who, in order to amuse the
gods, performed dances and plays, in which *Gandharvas*
and *Apsarasas* figured as actors and actresses.[2] These
performances, the legend says, were of three kinds :
(1) *nritta*, dances only ; (2) *nritya*, pantomimic dances
without dialogue ; (3) *natya*, pantomimic dances with
dialogue. In fact, these are the first three stages of
the scale through which dramatic acting has passed in
India as elsewhere. That this is so we find further
confirmed by the language. The verbal root *nrit, nat*,
signifies " to dance," but in the causative *nâtayati*
it means " to represent dramatically " ; *nâtya* means
" dancing, mimetics, scenic performance, dramatic art " ;

---

[1] *Mricchakatikâ* (earthenware, or toy, cart), which is attributed to King
Sûdraka, and which hitherto has been considered as the oldest Indian
drama known to us, now appears to be of a later date than Kâlidâsa.
Comp., *e.g.*, L. v. Schrœder : *Indiens Literatur u. Cultur.* S. Lévi : *Le
Théâtre Indien.* Paris, 1890. E. Senart : *Le Théâtre Indien (Revue des
deux Mondes*, 1891).

[2] *Gandharvas* were a kind of demi-gods, warlike and fond of women ; they
were sometimes represented in half-animal form ; at any rate they are posses-
sors of the divine horses, and are supposed to be identical with the centaurs
of the Greeks. The *Apsarasas* are the Indian houri, beautiful tempting
demi-goddesses, who delight the gods and saints with their songs and dances.

nata and *nâtaka* from the same root mean "an actor" (properly speaking, a dancer); the neuter *nâtaka* is "a play," especially the highest kind of play.[1]

Now, if it is clear for one thing that dramatic art in India, according to the general rule, began with dancing, it seems no less clear—in spite of contradictory statements from famous Indologists — that it was originally connected with divine worship. Even as early as the time of the *Vedas*, singing and dancing formed an essential part of Indian worship. Three ecclesiastical orders shared between them the ceremonies which were required to give effect to the sacrifice. The *Adhvaryus* performed the offering of the sacrifice, and on these occasions sometimes acted a real part, while the *Udgâtris* sang the obligatory hymns, which not unfrequently were quite dramatic in subject and form. The pantomimic part fell to the share of the *Hotris*; they performed a rhythmic dance round the altar, lifting their arms towards the sky, bowing towards the east, kneeling before the fire, and accompanying the ceremony with mute symbolic gestures, the meaning and detailed description of which is written in still-existing manuals for the priests. Everywhere in the oldest Indian literature dancing is mentioned as a principal item at the religious offerings, and even at the present day no Indian pagoda is without its *bayadera*, who performs a solemn dance as an introduction to all the festivals of the inhabitants.[2]

In Bengal a certain kind of popular plays, called

[1] L. v. Schrœder, *Indiens Lit. und Cultur*, p. 592.
[2] Mill, *History of British India*, vol. ii. p. 266, quoted by Du Méril, § 1, p. 181.

Yâtrâs, have survived up to the present day. The original meaning of *Yâtrâ* is "walk, speed," from the root *Ya*, to walk ; it also means "procession," and finally "plays acted at religious festivals and processions." These popular dramas generally represent events in the life of Krishna, the "God-man." Krishna is one of the incarnations of Vishnu ; his life on earth is told in a huge epic : *Mahâbhârata*.[1] For some time he lived as king of a people of herdsmen, and it is this part of his life and his love story with a herd-girl which forms the principal subject of the Yâtrâs.

Gîta-Govinda, a lyric-dramatic poem of the twelfth century, treats of the same subject. These festive plays contain, for the most part, lyric verses, some of which are sung, others recited. The dialogue is only worked out in a fragmentary way ; most of it is left to be improvised by the actors, as in the Italian comedy of masks ; the persons, too, are always the same : Krishna, his lady-love Râdhâ ; his father, his mother, the herd-girls, and the clown Nârada.

It seems natural to suppose that these popular religious plays mark an earlier stage of development in the Indian drama than the traditional art poems of the Middle Ages, and to draw the conclusion that ancient scenic art was closely connected with the worship of Vishnu. However, we do not yet possess a definite proof that this was so, whereas the mediæval drama still bears marks of its religious origin, not indeed in its contents, which are quite secular in character, but in some peculiar outward characteristics. For instance,

---

[1] Especially in the tenth book of *Bhâgavata-Purâna*.

every piece begins with a prayer or blessing, *Nândi*,[1] which has nothing whatever to do with the subject of the play; it is simply a religious exhortation. In *Sakuntalâ* it runs as follows:—

> "Isà preserve you! he who is revealed
> In these eight forms by man perceptible—
> Water, of all creation's works the first;
> The fire that bears on high the sacrifice
> Presented with solemnity to heaven;
> The priest, the holy offerer of gifts;
> The Sun and Moon, those two majestic orbs,
> Eternal marshallers of day and night;
> The subtle Ether, vehicle of sound
> Diffused throughout the boundless universe;
> The Earth, by sages called 'The place of birth
> Of all material essences and things';
> And Air, which giveth life to all that breathe."
>
> (Free translation by Monier Williams.)

The prayer, of course, ought to be said by a priest, a brahmin, but, as a rule, it is the stage manager himself who is charged with this office. He—and most likely the other actors as well—really belonged to the highest Indian cast, the brahmins. That the prayer, at the time of the classical drama, was only a conventional form, seems evident from the somewhat irreverent words spoken before the performance of the *Toy Cart*[2] by the manager to the reciter (in this case, we see, they were not identical): "Enough of these irrelevant remarks, which only whet the curiosity of the assembly."

But even though we may succeed in proving by evidence that the Indian drama was of religious origin, we are not very much the wiser. The great gap in the development between the original ecclesiastical play

---

[1] The real meaning of the word is, "what pleases gods and men.'
[2] *Mricchakatikâ.*

and the regular classical drama remains as unexplained and inexplicable as ever. How is it that a literature extending over a few centuries can be entirely preserved, while of the dramatic literature belonging to the preceding period of nearly a thousand years' duration, not a single drama remains? That earlier dramas existed is a fact sufficiently proved by the pieces we know at present. Thus, for instance, in the introduction of Kâlidasâ's *The King and the Bayadera*, we find the following sentence: " Do you really mean to pass by the works of the far-renowned poets of old time, Bhâsa, Saumillas, and others, and to prefer a work by the now living Kâlidâsa?" And in the prologue of *Vikramorvaçî* the manager says: " This assembly is tired of never seeing anything but subjects that have been treated by the poets of former times. Therefore I will show them a new play named *Vikrama* and *Urvaçî*, the author of which is Kâlidâsa."

Moreover, several of the numerous dramatic handbooks possessed by the Indians are no doubt of more ancient date than any of the dramas preserved, an unmistakable sign of the earlier existence of a developed drama, for no people, however philosophically inclined, can be imagined to have written a theory of an art before that art was practised.

In order to explain this remarkable gap in the development, several hypotheses have been suggested by famous Sanscritologists, but this is not the proper place for explaining them, especially as none of them seems yet to have hit the mark. I will only *en passant* mention Senart's theory that, previously to the written classical dramas, there must have existed *unwritten plays transmitted verbally*, which furnished material for the written theoretical works. In fact, Indian literature possesses an abundance of manuals, not only on dramaturgy and the theories of other arts, but on nearly every subject that can be treated theoretically. There is no branch of art, no trade, no occupation, which has not its detailed systematic theories, to such an extent that we even find complete guides for thieves and courtesans. The numerous dramatic text-books do not differ much from each other ; they are all based on the same rules and tradition ; they only concern themselves about outward forms, the surface and appearance of scenic matters, and have nothing whatever to do with the philosophy and the æsthetics of the drama.

According to these text-books [1] the Indians divide all dramatic fictions into two principal categories : 1. the so - called *rûpaka* or higher drama ; 2. *uparûpaka* or lower drama. The former again is subdivided into ten species, the latter into eighteen ; this makes a total of *twenty-eight*. This astounding multitude of varieties is the outcome of an equally astounding childish formalism in Indian theorists, for the differences between the species are based on nothing but indifferent details. The Indians carry their pedantry and their mania for classification so far that, with regard to certain plays—the supernatural—they not only prescribe the number of acts, but even *to the minute* the length of each act.

The drama which ranks highest—the first among the so-called *rûpakas* — is the *nâtaka*, the drama *par*

---

[1] One of the oldest and best of them bears the title of *Daça Rûpaka*, a description of the ten modes of theatrical composition.

excellence. The subject of a *nâtaka* must always be a well-known important event taken from mythology or history; within this limit, however, free scope is left to the author's imagination. Only persons of high rank or distinction may be represented. The hero must be a prince like Dushyanta (in *Sakuntalâ*), a demigod like Râma, or a deity like Krishna. The only admissible motive of action is love or heroism, rendered in sublime and delicate language. The number of acts is limited to the maximum of ten and the minimum of five. However, the sublime character of these plays does not exclude comic figures and merry scenes. A sad ending is absolutely forbidden in these, as in all kinds of Indian dramas. Among the twenty - eight different varieties none resembles our tragedies, for, in spite of the pessimism of the Hindoos, they never allowed a scenic performance to leave a painful or sad impression on the spectators. To represent a homicide on the stage would be considered indecent : in the *Toy Cart* it is only allowed because it is a sham. Coarse, violent effects are altogether forbidden, as being offensive to the dignity of the stage and to the delicate feeling of a distinguished audience. In serious plays, for instance, hostile challenges, curses or national defeats, are excluded, and, in comic pieces, biting, scratching, kissing, eating, sleeping, bathing or anointing, as well as the matrimonial act. However, in the plays known to us, these rules are not strictly kept.

While *Sakuntalâ* belongs to the highest class as a distinct *nâtaka*, the *Toy Cart* offers an example of a *prakarana*, belonging to the second class, the *rûpaka* category. The *rûpaka* is very like the *nâtaka*, except that its subject must be a fictitious action of everyday life. Its chief characters, however, must belong to the higher classes of society : the hero must have the rank of a brahmin, a minister, or a great merchant. The heroine may be a young girl of good family, but also—as in the *Toy Cart*— a courtesan, a class of women whose position, as shown, for example, in the play just mentioned, was much more respectable in those times than in modern society. Love is considered the most suitable motive of the plot.

In the category of *uparûpaka* the *nâtikâ* stands as number one, but this class differs in nothing from the *nâtaka* (the first class of the highest category) except that the number of acts must not exceed four. A rather more important division of the *uparûpaka* is the *trotaka*, which is allowed five, seven, eight, or nine acts, and in which the scene is laid partly on earth, partly in heaven. To this class belongs *Urvaçi*,[1] the third piece of Kâlidâsa's, which is still preserved.

It would be an idle task, however, to enumerate all the twenty-eight divisions. Among their number we find the fantastic four-act drama, in which all kinds of magic tricks impress the spectator rather unpleasantly : the war-play in one act; the supernatural play in three acts, in which the scene is laid among gods and demons. But in reality the pieces we know can easily be classed into five categories : 1. the great heroic drama, *nâtaka ;* 2. the domestic play, *prakarana ;* 3. the smaller heroic drama, *nâtikâ ;* 4. the farce, *prahasana ;* and 5. the monologue.[2] Among these the farce is not the least interesting

---

[1] L. v. Schrœder : *Indiens Lit. u. Cult*, pp. 503 ff.
[2] Sylvain Lévi : *Le Théâtre indien.*

category.   With coarse jokes, often combined with the grossest indecencies, the learned brahmins—the only literary caste—kick over the traces, generally choosing members of their own class as butts for their jests.

Outside these five divisions stands a rather remarkable allegorical drama belonging to the end of the eleventh century of our era, which in many points reminds us of our mediæval moralities ; its title is, *The rising of the moon of wisdom—prabodhaçandrodaya—* and its object is a glorification of the theology of Vishnu. For this purpose a number of personified virtues and vices appear on the boards.   The heroes of the play are: mighty King Error and noble King Wisdom.   King Error reigns in Benares ; at his court and in his country his faithful subjects, Selfishness, Voluptuousness, Hypocrisy, Heresy, and Cupidity carry on their business, while good King Wisdom and all his partisans—the human virtues —are driven from the country in disgrace.   But then the prophecy is spread that if King Wisdom will wed Revelation—the orthodox religion—the outcome of this union will be True Knowledge, and the government of King Error will be overthrown.   The struggle to bring about this alliance, by which the good cause will prevail in the end, forms the subject of the play.[1]

---

[1] Nowadays a similar kind of moralities is acted in Thibetan convents. These performances take place once a year, and their subject is the temptation of a faithful one by the principle of evil, his victorious resistance and final recompense by Buddha.   The actors of these moralities wear masks.   The mask of the faithful one resembles a llama, that of the evil principle is red ; the wicked female spirit, who accompanies the evil one, has long plaits like the Thibetan women ; while the good angel who helps the faithful one wears a turban.   Buddha wears a mask with three eyes.—Schlagintweit : *Bericht an die geographische Gesellschaft in Berlin,* February 6th, 1858.

It is not dramas of this kind, however, which to European readers have created the success of the Indian theatre. The Indian drama, like a magic word, unfolds before our eyes a bright sunny landscape of flourishing lianas, sweet-smelling mango trees, soft-flowing rivers, at which the light-footed gazelles quench their thirst, and on whose banks high palm trees nod their tops, while brown love-seeking maidens play on the lawn and adorn themselves with lotus flowers, admired by the bold eyes of fairy kings, and protected by the wise admonitions of pious hermits. All this natural poetry was revealed to Europe just when it was getting tired of the cut and dried eighteenth-century poetry, when the idyll was becoming the fashion, and when romanticism was spreading its roots in the soil of literature. No wonder that this exotic plant was received with enthusiasm ; its colour was so fresh, its smell so sweet, that even the sharpest minds forgot to criticise and failed to notice the hothouse atmosphere which had produced this fruit : Goethe's above-quoted distich bears sufficient witness to this. Romanticism revelled in palms and lotuses. Rückert transferred the Indian lyric spirit to German poetry, and Gérard de Nerval—the super-romantic poet—attempted, though without success, to interest Parisians in the very play which of late years, under the name of *Vasantasênâ*, has made its triumphal entry on to most European stages.

In spite of the charm which the best Indian plays insensibly exercise on first acquaintance on a receptive mind, it cannot be denied that all that is known to us of Indian dramatic literature does not contain a single work fraught with that mighty power, which by its passion, its depth of thought and profound knowledge of human nature, irresistibly carries us away and compels our veneration. The Indian drama breathes a gentle grace, which produces a sensation of quiet ease in the reader or spectator, and its passion seldom goes beyond a sensual, somewhat indolent love, which derives its greatest attraction from the description of nature in which it is framed.

II

Outward Conditions—The Play-hall and its Decorations—Theoretical and Practical Instruction of the Actors—Difficulty of their Art—Dialects —Mimic Play—Social Position of Actors.

IF the stage were bound to satisfy approximately the requirements of the drama in the matter of decorative art, the Indian theatre ought to possess a more complicated machinery than any modern European theatre has ever produced. The Indian stage, for one thing, is frequently supposed to represent several different places simultaneously. Thus, for instance, in the second act of the *Toy Cart* the scene is laid at the same time outside and inside the house of Vasantasênâ ; this might perhaps be managed even with the means accessible in primitive times, but in the following act the difficulties become insuperable. To begin with, a servant appears in a room of Cârudattâ's house ; immediately after, there is a conversation between Cârudattâ and Maitrêya, from which we gather that they are on their way home from an excursion ; a moment later they arrive at the house and enter it, after which the scene is again supposed to take place in the inner part of the house. The next scene represents a burglary in the same dwelling. Thieves have worked a hole in a garden wall, and are now going to break through the wall, in the very place where, a moment before, a door was supposed to be. This work is described in detail. The ninth act begins as follows :—

(*Enter an officer of justice.*)

OFFICER.

I am commanded to prepare the benches in this hall for the judges (*arranges them*). All is ready for their reception, the floor is swept and the seats are placed, and I have only now to inform them that all is ready (*going*). (Wilson.)

Finally in the fourth act there is a long scene with a picturesque description of Maitrêya's walk through the palace of Vasantasênâ. The girl shows him round and says :—

ATTENDANT.

This is the outer door, sir.

MAITRÊYA.

A very pretty entrance indeed. The threshold is very neatly coloured, well swept and watered. . . . Over the doorway is a lofty arch of ivory ; above it again wave flags dyed with safflower. On either side, the capitals of the door-posts support elegant crystal flower-pots in which young mango trees are springing up. The door-panels are of gold, stuck, like the stout breast of a demon, with studs of adamant. . . .

ATTENDANT.

This leads to the first court.   Enter, sir, enter.

(*They enter the first court.*)

MAITRÊYA.

Bless me, why here is a line of palaces, as white as the moon, as the conch, as the stalk of the water-lily. . . . The porter dozes in an easy-chair, as stately as a brahmin deep in the Vedas. . . . Proceed.

ATTENDANT.

That is the second court.   Enter.

MAITRÊYA.

Oh, here are the stables; the carriage oxen are in good case, pampered with jawasa,[1] I declare, and straw and oil cakes are ready for them; their horns are bright with grease; here we have a buffalo snorting indignantly, like a brahmin of high caste whom somebody has affronted. . . . Proceed.

ATTENDANT.

This, sir, is the third gateway.

(*They enter the third court.*)

MAITRÊYA.

Oh, this is the public court, where the young bucks of Ujayin assemble; these are their seats, I suppose, etc.

Evidently no attempts have been made to solve these difficult problems.   It is a very great question also whether, as some authors have suggested, the stage is sometimes divided into two compartments, one of which

[1] Wilson's note : a species of hedge arum.

is supposed to represent the inside of a house, the other the yard in front of it. Realistic stage arrangements have probably never been attempted at all, and shutting doors, entering a room, etc., have merely been simulated by the actors. This opinion seems to be confirmed by the fact that, while we meet with very numerous and detailed instructions with regard to acting—sometimes even indicating that such and such an action is only shammed[1]—there are no rubrics whatever containing instructions about scenic decorations or the localities to be represented.

So it seems natural to suppose that it was left entirely to the performer's mimic and descriptive powers to give his audience the right idea of the locality to be represented at any given moment.

We lack positive information about the outward conditions of the theatre, but we may take for granted that the performances were of a sporadic incidental character. As a fact, most of the plays we know were acted to celebrate national or religious festivals : for instance, *Sakuntalâ* and *Ratnâvali*[2] at the "Celebration of Spring" (*Vasantakîyâtrâ*), and *The Three Dramas of Bhavabhûti, Mâlatî and Mâdhava, The History of Râma*,[3] as well as *The End of Râma's History*,[4] at the " Festival of the Sun-god," Siva. There was, therefore, no stationary theatre at all, but the performances took place either in some suitable hall—supposing it was the king or some other distinguished person who gave

---

[1] Compare, *e.g.*, *Sakuntalâ*, in which the driver illustrates "the speed of the carriage by his movements."

[2] *The String of Pearls*, a piece attributed to Çriharsha.

[3] *Mahâviracarita.*   [4] *Uttararâmacarita.*

the festival—or on a stage hurriedly constructed for
the occasion, in which case the strolling managers,
sûtradhâras, with their companies, paid the expenses.

In an old work on the theory of music, the *Sangî-
taratnâkara*, we read a description of the above-mentioned kind of play-hall; though it was intended for
musical performances, we can scarcely be mistaken in
supposing that play-halls were arranged in a similar way.
It is described as follows :—" The room in which dances
are performed must be spacious and beautifully decorated.
The canvas-roofed hall must be provided with richly
ornamented pillars, and adorned all over with garlands
of flowers. The master of the house is seated in the
middle of the hall on an elevated throne ; on his right
hand great dignitaries are placed, on his left his nearest
relations, and behind them State or domestic officers.
Female attendants with fans and screens are grouped
round the governor, while staff-bearers, who maintain
order, and armed guards, occupy the posts allotted to
them. When all are seated, the artists enter and sing
some songs, after which the first dancing girl appears
from behind a curtain, bows to the assembly, throws
flowers to the spectators, and begins dancing."

From this description we see how the hall was
decorated, and how the higher classes were placed ; but
it tells us nothing about the stage, except that it had a
curtain which concealed the performers till it was their
turn to appear before the public. But even this drapery
was not a stage curtain in our sense of the word —
separating the stage from the spectators ; such a curtain
did not exist in Indian play-halls. The Indian curtain

only concealed the background of the stage and the dressing-room.[1] This is seen, for instance, from King Agnimitra's speech in Kâlidâsa's *The King and the Bayadera*, after Malâvikâ has danced before him :—

Have done with this limiting of your power. For, now, I consider her disappearance behind the curtain to be like the obscuration of the prosperity of my two eyes, like the end of the great feast of my heart, like the closing of the door of joy (C. H. Fawney).

This drapery is called *Yavanikâ* ("the Greek curtain"), from *Yavana* = "Ionian," "Greek": a name which is remarkable in so far as it is quoted as the principal support of the opinion which supposes the Indian drama to have originated under Greek influence.

We will not enter more closely into this question ; too little light has been thrown upon it as yet, and it is too risky for one who is not a master of Sanscrit to side with any party, so long as it is a standing point of controversy among learned authorities. But so much we can assert—that, while Greek influence on Indian culture is in many respects unquestionable and important, as in architecture, numismatics, astronomy and, perhaps, legendary lore, the influence—if any—which the Greek theatre has had on the Indian, is so trifling and has left so few marks with regard to the subjects we are treating—stage conditions and dramatic art—that it would seem to begin and end with "the Greek curtain," and that we need not scruple to leave it out of consideration.

[1] *Nepathya.*

As for the stage itself, it is evident—at least, at the time of the classical drama—that it consisted merely of a raised platform at the back of the hall, without a front curtain and without any decorations but a piece of drapery forming the background.   Here the actors moved backwards and forwards ; those that were unoccupied retired to the back of the stage and did not come forward till it was their turn to act.   This at least seems to be indicated by the technical terms for " enter " and " exit," *praviçati* and *nishkrâmati*, meaning respectively " he advances " and " he retires." [1]

Sometimes, no doubt, the objects and properties prescribed in the play were really produced.   Thus we scarcely see how the presentation of real carriages could be avoided in the sixth act of the *Toy Cart* ; the very plot is constructed on Vasantasênâ's mistaking one of the two carriages for the other, and in some of the stage directions we find the carriage repeatedly mentioned as an object really used on the stage.   On the whole, we feel sure, very little fuss was made about properties ; in this respect also it was left to the actor's skill to create the illusion.   This cannot be said with regard to costumes, which seem to have been gorgeous wherever a display of attire was required, and as a rule the costumes harmonised well with the character of the part, though—judging from occasional passages in the plays—first lovers even then indulged in a tendency to excessive costliness of dress. [2]

That the Indians laid great stress on professional train-

---

[1] Ed. du Méril : *La Comédie ancienne*, i. p. 183 f.

[2] " This girl, who is bedisened with gold from top to toe, like the chief of a troop of comedians about to act a new play." *Toy Cart*, Sc. 21.

ing is evident from many passages in their plays. In the introduction to *Sakuntalâ* we read :—

"No skill in acting can I deem complete,
Till from the wise the actor gain applause :
Know that the heart e'en of the truly skilful
Shrinks from too boastful confidence in self."

(Free transl. by Monier Wilson.)

And in the *Toy Cart* we find the following words about Vasantasênâ : "Yes, it may be she has been taught to disguise her voice in the way of her profession, both for the purpose of deception and the articulation of the gamut."

During the stage-apprenticeship theoretical instruction is combined with practical teaching. As may be gathered from what we have said about the Indian taste for systematic classification, the text-books contain no end of complicated rules and divisions which had to be impressed on the poor actors by their teachers, and not always, we feel sure, by gentle means. According to these rules scenic art has *four means of representation* : 1. *movement*, 2. *voice*, 3. *costume*, 4. *expression*. Distinction is further made between eight *impressions—rasas*—which this art can produce : 1. the *erotic*, 2. the *comical*, 3. the *pathetic*, 4. the *tragic*, 5. the *heroic*, 6. the *awful*, 7. the *hateful*, 8. the *miraculous*. A similar number of *states of mind—bhâvas*—are attributed to the interpreter (and the author).[1] The latter category is subjective, the former objective.

---

[1] *Rasas* and *bhâvas* are indeed synonyms which apply to all poetry, but they are specially applicable to dramatic art. Comp. Sénart : *Le Théâtre indien*, pp. 91 ff., and Klein, iii. pp. 69 ff.

But the eight *bhâvas* have two sub-divisions : *a.* the *changing* (*passing*) *states*, such as fear, depression, indolence, etc., thirty-three in all ; *b.* the *physical states*, viz., the physical means of showing the different states of mind, as trembling, tears, etc. But this is not all : the two subjective sub-divisions of *bhâvas* presuppose similar objective ones : the feelings and circumstances which produce the first-mentioned *bhâvas*, and are called *vibhâvas* ; and the different states of body and mind which are a consequence of them, and are called *anubhâvas*.

The parts to be acted are classified in the same circumstantial way. The hero, *Nâyaka*, alone is conceived in forty-eight different characters, which again are divided into four principal groups : 1. the merry careless hero, *Dhîralalita* ; 2. the generous, virtuous hero, *Dhîraçanta* ; 3. the brave but prudent hero, *Dhîrodâtta* ; 4. the ardent, ambitious, proud and zealous hero, *Dhîroddhata*.

Among other figures characteristic of the Indian play we find *Pîthamardha*, the friend and confidant of the hero, and *Pratinâyaka*, the villain, his antagonist, as well as the so-called *Vidûshaka*, the comical parallel of the hero, his constant companion and helper in his love-affairs, but not his servant. The *Vidûshaka* is always a brahmin, a sort of shabby, half-starved fellow, who generally lives at the hero's expense, either as a kind of court-fool—like the lazy and greedy Mâdhavya in *Sakuntalâ*, or as a friend and helpmate, like the silly but good-natured Maitrêya in the *Toy Cart*. Another not so well defined character is the *Vita*. He is the supple courtier, who publicly praises his master's follies, but in secret laughs at them and scorns them, a high-class parasite, who nevertheless is occasionally bold enough to throw aside his reserve and tell his master the truth. An Indian verse in the Calcutta edition of *Mricchakatikâ* characterises the *Vita* in the following way : " The *Vita* is cunning, clever in some kind of art, courteous to prostitutes, eloquent, pleasant and much appreciated in society." However, neither the *Vidûshaka* nor the *Vita* shine much by their wit ; their jokes are rather insipid. As a rule, comic power is not the strong point of the Indian drama.

The female parts, which in India—contrary to the custom in other tropical countries as well as in Greece —were performed by women,[1] were generally classed according to the relations in which they stood to some man : his wife, another man's wife or daughter, an independent woman, etc. These classes again were subdivided according to their age, and these divisions and subdivisions amounted to as many as 384. It was an inviolable rule that no love-relation of a man to another man's wife could be made the subject of a plot, a rule which would be somewhat embarrassing to modern dramatists.

In spite of the apparently great abundance of characters, the tasks which the actors had to solve were not really distinguished by marked characteristics or psychological depth. The types are much the same in all plays, and the psychology is very superficial. It is

---

[1] There are exceptions, however. Old women and nuns were sometimes performed by men. Thus in the prologue of *Mâlati and Mâdhava* an actor says : " Our first actor is going to appear disguised as Kamandarî, an old Buddhistic beggar-woman, together with one of her female apprentices, Avalokitâ ; it is I who perform this part."

quite an exception to meet as peculiar and pronounced a character as Sansthânaka in the *Toy Cart*, who is a wicked swaggering fool, and at the same time brutishly sly. Otherwise we find that, within the principal categories, such as heroes, lovers, comic figures, the individual characters are scarcely distinguished from each other by anything but the outward conditions under which they appear, and we have reason to suppose, at least with regard to smaller companies, that they had a collection of stock plays with standing characters, like the Italian mask-comedies.[1]

Thus, the Indian actor could dispense with deep study of human nature; but, on the other hand, he was bound to possess a high degree of *practical* skill, and, above all, a perfect mastery of the different languages and dialects of his country.

One peculiarity of the Indian drama is that—besides being composed in prose as well as in verse—it is written in two different languages, Sanscrit and Prâkrit. Sanscrit was the classical, learned, literary language, a kind of high Indian, which was not used in everyday talk, only in writing and in rhetoric. " Its position may be compared to that of Latin in the Middle Ages."[2] The popular colloquial tongue with its different dialects was Prâkrit. The outward relation between the two languages may be compared to that between Italian and Latin. Prâkrit is a softened Sanscrit. Thus in Prâkrit

---

[1] Comp. Ed. du Méril : *op. cit.* p. 193 and p. 6. Comp. also the standing characters in the afore-mentioned *Yâtrâs*.

[2] E. Senart : *op. cit.* p. 88. Comp. Sórensen : *On the Position of Sanskrit in the General Development of Languages in India.* Copenhagen, 1894, pp. 244 ff.

Sakuntalâ is called *Saundalâ; Dushyanta* is *Dussanda; Prijamvada* is *Piamvada; lavona* (salt) is *lona; sabha* (assembly) is *saha*.[1]

Now, in the plays the principal male characters—gods and dignitaries of the two highest castes (brahmins and warriors)—talked Sanscrit, while all women (even goddesses), children, lower-class people, and the merrymaker (though always a brahmin) talked Prâkrit. The latter tongue again was subdivided into a number of different dialects which were used according to a regular system, into the laws and details of which we have not penetrated. The most important dialect is the so-called Çaurasenî, which was spoken by the heroine and other prominent female characters, as well as by the *Vidûshaka*, and in the prologue by the stage manager. Royal Court officials speak another principal dialect, Mâgadhî, low comedians Prâcyâ. Sometimes the same person uses one dialect in prose, another in verse.

Why this number of dialects—sometimes as many as seven or eight—were used is still an open question. Perhaps it was in imitation of real life, though it seems more likely that it was a conventional way of showing the spectators the character of the part, as well as the social position of each actor.

It is evident, at any rate, that this point added greatly to the difficulty of dramatic art, and laid a heavy burden on the shoulders of the actors. Moreover, they had to be trained in singing and dancing, or at least in mimicry.

We know that music formed a very important item of Indian performances, so important that these plays

[1] Ernst Meier : *Sakuntalâ.* Introduction, p. xxvi.

might perhaps most appropriately be compared to our so-called comic operas, viz., operettas intermixed with dialogue. Indian music, however, is still to a great extent *terra incognita*; it has not yet been made the object of historical and critical research by experts, and from the plays themselves very few conclusions can be drawn. Besides, it does not enter into the plan of the present work to study the details of this branch of dramatic performance. As for the by-play, the mute part of dramatic acting, it may be said with even more reason, and not only concerning India, that hitherto it has been left without scientific exposition. Here and there, however, we find indications in the plays; and, though they are very far from exhausting the matter, they help us to form an idea of the place which dumb-show occupied on the Indian stage.

That the authors attributed great importance to supplementary gestures and movements is clearly testified by the numerous hints which are found in most of the plays, and which are always well considered and correct in their effect—even more so than in modern European authors. Here we give only a few examples taken from the first act of *Sakuntalâ*.

[*King Dushyanta is chasing a gazelle.*]

THE KING.

. . . Now, Charioteer, see me kill the deer!

(*Takes aim.*)

A VOICE BEHIND THE SCENES.

Hold, O King! This deer belongs to our hermitage. Kill it not! kill it not!

CHARIOTEER.

Great King, some hermits have stationed themselves so as to screen the antelope at the very moment of its coming within range of your arrow.

KING (*hastily*).

Then stop the horses.

CHARIOTEER.

I obey.   (*Stops the chariot.*)
(*Enter a hermit and two others with him.*)

HERMIT (*raising his hand*).

This deer, King, belongs to our hermitage.   Kill it not! kill it not!

[*The king is talking to the three hermit girls, and has questioned them about Sakuntalâ's parentage.*]

ANASUYA.

Well, then, it happened that Viswamitra, gazing on the bewitching beauty of that nymph at a season when spring was in its glory —— (*Stops short and appears confused.*)

KING.

The rest may be easily divined.   Sakuntalâ, then, is the offspring of the nymph.

ANASUYA.

Just so.

KING.

It is quite intelligible.

How could a mortal to such charms give birth?
The lightning's radiance flashes not from earth.
>   (*Sakuntalâ remains modestly seated with down-*
>   *cast eyes.*)

(*Aside.*) And so my desire has really scope for its
indulgence.   Yet I am still distracted by doubts, re-
membering the pleasantry of her female companions
respecting her wish for a husband.

Prijamvada.

(*Looking with a smile at Sakuntalâ, and then turning*
towards the King.)   You seem desirous, sir, of asking
something further.   (*Sakuntalâ makes a chiding gesture*
with her finger.)

Compared, for instance, with the total lack of stage
directions as to gesture in the Shakesperian plays, we
may safely conclude that Indian dramatic art was anything but casual or improvised, for, insignificant as
the above hints—chosen at random—may appear to
the ordinary reader, an expert immediately feels that
they seem so natural only because they always hit the
mark.   How expressive this little parenthesis: "Sakuntalâ makes a chiding gesture with her finger"! it paints
better than words could do Sakuntalâ's confusion and
annoyance at her friend's indiscretion.

But sometimes also mimic action had to work more
independently.   I will just mention a few peculiarities
which soon strike an attentive reader.   The authors do
not like to relate events which have taken place before

the eyes of the spectators. If such information is unavoidable, it is given by signs only, *i.e.*, the person concerned expresses by dumb - show what somebody else has to learn. Thus, for instance, in the *Toy Cart* (concerning some ornaments, the history of which is known to the spectators, but not to the persons who ask questions about them) :—

MAITRÊYA.

It is the same ! I swear it, as I am a brahmin.

CÂRUDATTA.

I am glad of it.

MAITRÊYA.

Shall I ask how they came by it ?

CÂRUDATTA.

Why not ? (*Maitrêya asks the attendant, who whispers to him.*) What are you saying there? Am I not to hear?

MAITRÊYA (*whispers to Cârudatta*).
Now I will tell you.

There is another feature characteristic of the Indian as well as of the Chinese and the Japanese drama: where the author lacks words for painting great anxiety or violent passion, he simply makes his character faint ; that is to say, he leaves it to the dumb-show of the actor to express what words would be unable to paint. Thus in the fourth act of the *Toy Cart*, where Sarvîlaka tells Vasantasênâ and Madânikâ about his breaking into the

house of Cârudatta, without knowing that he is loved by
Vasantasênâ, he says : "I was informed then that near
the Bazar resided the chief of his tribe, one Cârudatta."

Here the tale is interrupted by the following brief
stage-direction : "*Vasantasênâ and Madânikâ faint.*"
Of course, it must have depended upon the actresses
whether this scene was to appear ludicrous—it certainly
appears in this light to the reader—or not. That the
author desires very expressive acting is shown by the
following speech of Sarvîlaka :—

"Madânikâ revive! what ails the wench?

Her limbs are all unstrung, her looks are wild," etc.

No doubt all their mimic art was built on a system
of symbolic gestures ; it was carefully studied as an
independent accomplishment, and taught by a staff of
skilful teachers,[1] among whom we find the name of
Buddha, the great reformer himself. We confess that
our knowledge of the symbolic part of this system is
almost nil. Only a few involuntary movements, which
recur constantly in all plays, are specially pointed out
as ominous. A throb of the right arm or eye was considered a good omen for a man, a bad one for a woman.
A throb of the left arm or eye, on the contrary, augured
well for a woman, badly for a man.[2]

However, in several pieces we meet with independent

---

[1] "Listen, king! I learned the art of dramatic acting from a good
teacher. I have given lessons in the art. I have been favoured by the king
and the queen" (*King and Bayadera*, Act i., Sc. 14).

[2] "My right arm throbs as I receive the weapon. Fortune is friendly
to me. I am safe" (*Toy Cart*, Act vii., p. 113).

"I know the reason of my festal attire. Nevertheless my heart trembles
like water in the leaf of a lotus. Moreover my left eye throbs" (*King
and Bayadera*, Act v., p. 75).

little interludes, which apparently have no other purpose than to exhibit the performer's skill. We have already mentioned the little episode with the bee in the first act of *Sakuntalâ*, and a scene in *The King and the Bayadera* gives us some idea of the manner in which such a part is performed. In the play *Mâlavikâ*, the actress who performs the love scene has to exhibit her skill in mimicry before the king ; she begins by singing this little poem :—

" My beloved is hard to obtain, be thou without hope with respect to him, oh my heart ! Ha ! the outer corner of my left eye throbs somewhat : how is this man, seen after a long time, to be obtained ? My lord, consider that I am devoted to thee with ardent longing." (As she sings she *goes through a pantomime* expressive of the sentiment.) Then follows a critique of the performance by a nun who has been present, and she describes the dance as follows :—

" All was blameless and in accordance with the rules of art, for the meaning was completely expressed by her limbs, which were full of language ; the movement of her feet was in perfect time, she exactly represented the sentiments ; the acting was gentle, based upon the different forms of feeling ; in the successive exhibition of their various shades emotion trod on the heels of emotion—it was a vivid picture of a series of passions."

Such mimic intermezzi, which evidently formed a chief attraction of the plays, were often introduced where they had nothing whatever to do with the subject of the drama, and where they would seem more likely to interrupt than to intensify the suspense of the spectators.

Thus, for instance, in the burglar scene of the *Toy Cart* (Act iii.), where the thief is suddenly and without reasonable purpose stung by a serpent, and gives mimic expression to the pains caused by the poison; and finally, having tied up his finger with his sacrificial string (this thief is a brahmin), he declares: "'Tis well again—I must get on." Further on in the same scene, frightened by the lamp-light, he says: "Softly: the light will betray me. I have the light-seeking insect to put it out. I must cast it into the lamp. (*Takes out the insect.*) Place and time requiring, let this insect fly. It hovers round the wick—with the wind of its wings the flame is extinguished."

Obviously there is no lamp, either burning or extinguished, much less a light-seeking insect; the whole scene is fictitious, and invented in order to show off the actor's skill in mimicry, and also to supply the local colour, which is not produced by scenic decoration.

A similar, even more detailed, scene is acted by the charioteer Sthâvaraka in the sixth act of the same play.

(*Outside.   Enter Sthâvaraka with a carriage.*)

I am ordered by the king's brother-in-law, my master, to take this vehicle with all speed to the old flower garden, Pushpakarandaka. Come up, come up. (*Looking.*) Why, the road is blocked with country carts. Holla there! get out of the way. What says he; whose carriage is it? Sansthânaka's, the king's brother-in-law; quick, quick! clear the road. (*Drives on.*) Who should that be that looked at me so curiously, and then stole off down another road, like an unlucky gambler that runs away from the table-keepers. No matter; I must get on. Holloa, you, out of the way there! What! Come and give you a turn of the wheel; it sticks, does it? It is very likely that the king's brother-in-law's man shall assist you to a twist of the wheel. Oh, it is a poor, miserable rustic, and alone too. Well, I will lend you a hand. This is Cârudatta's postern door. I can have the carriage here in the meantime, so, stop there, I will be with you.

(*Exit, leaving the carriage at the door.*)

Indian dramatic art is at the same time profound and superficial; superficial, in so far that it does not enter into any depth of feeling, but only represents light or gentle sentiments; profound, because it works out every detail with untiring perseverance and accuracy, and claims a very careful training of its performers.

Actors—at least at the time of the classical drama —formed an independent class. Several passages in the plays seem to indicate this; for instance, these words by the manager in the prologue of *Ratnâvali*:—

" I must point out to you that for our part we have some experience in theatrical matters, wherefore I hope that the favourable opportunity offered to me here of appearing before such a distinguished assembly, as well as such a precious poetical work, skilful actors, and similar means of pleasing you, will procure me all the benefit I can desire."

We also see from this speech that it was the manager who bore the risk of the performances, but he was not necessarily the performer of the principal part. His title,

as we have said, was *Sutradhâra*, a word which is interpreted in different ways, most frequently as the person
who superintends the construction and arrangement of
the theatre.   A more plausible hypothesis, however,
explains it as being borrowed from the managers of
strolling puppet-shows, and meaning "the wire-puller."
According to this version the Sutradhâra is the
manager of the company who studies the plays,
instructs the actors, and at the same time bears the
financial responsibility.[1]

As to the social condition of actors, the statements
are very contradictory.   Some of them tell us how
highly they were considered, how frequently they belonged to the highest caste (the brahmins), how well-to-
do, etc.   Others say that they stood outside the castes,
like wild swine, serpents and reptiles; one of their
names was *Kuçîlava*, which means "a person of bad
morals," and in a record of the seventh century we read:
"butchers, fishers, *actors*, hangmen, and scavengers are
turned out of the town and shown a place where they
may live.   When entering or leaving villages, they must
keep to the left of the road."[2]

It is possible, however, that these apparently contradictory statements are both equally true.   It is evident
that there were two classes of actors in India : the one,
distinguished, high bred, well instructed and esteemed,
lived in the large towns, at court, acted high classical
dramas, were friends with poets and philosophers, and

[1] Shankar Pandit : *Vikramorvaçi*, notes, p. 4, quot. by L. v. Schrœder,
op. cit. p. 600.

[2] Hiouen-thsang : *Mémoires sur les Contrées occidentales*, vol. i. p. 66,
Julien's translation.   Quoted by Ed. du Méril, *op. cit.* i. p. 18, n. 3.

enjoyed consideration at court; the other, poor despised vagabonds, travelled from village to village, playing their wretched, shamelessly indecent farces; their lives were scarcely more decent than their plays, and they were shunned as gipsies used to be in Europe, so that decent people avoided walking on the same side of the street, for fear of touching these unclean animals. Now, supposing that the favourable accounts refer to the high-class actors and the depreciating descriptions to the low-class, I think the right light is thrown on this somewhat obscure question. At any rate we may no doubt take it for granted that in India actors as a class stood higher than in other Asiatic countries, and that their art was nobler and more refined; or, in other words, what in those countries was only an entertainment or amusement of the crowd, in India was raised to the sphere of real art.

THE GREEK THEATRE

I

THE DRAMA

Origin of Greek Dramatic Art from the Dionysiac Festivals—The Bacchic Processions and Goat-songs—Phallus Worship—Tragedy and Satyr Plays—Thespis and his Reforms—Forms and Types of the Classic Tragedy—Origin and Development of Comedy—Political Plays and the Mixed Drama.

IF any theatre is autochthonous, certainly the Greek must be so designated. Scarcely any other people has produced a more original and more national drama. Yet in its origin and development Greek dramatic art resembles that of other countries, not only in the fact of its originating in religious festivals, but also in the nature of these festivals and sacrificial ceremonies, which recall to our minds what we know about divine cult among primitive nations. We meet with the same bloody human sacrifices, the same secret societies with their mystic initiations and their savage nature-worship, the same dances and songs, the same disguises and masks. It is naturally difficult to find out the original purpose of secret societies, but there does not seem to have been any essential difference, for instance, between the great association of the Areoi in the South Sea Islands and the Eleusinian Mysteries or the Cabeiric corporation in the Isle of Samothrace. They were religious societies for mutual support, with mysterious and gloomy ceremonies of admission, which, while well qualified to inspire their members with horror and deter them from breaking their connection with the society, were at the same time combined with merry feasts, at which drinking and singing were carried on for days and nights in succession.

The Greeks were a pleasure-seeking people, and their festivals were numerous. They had no weekly day of rest like our Sunday or the Sabbath of the Jews. Still, they did not forget their gods, and each of their principal deities had its festival, and was worshipped in its own particular way. Prayers, ablutions, fasts and sacrifices alternated with orgies, games, songs and dances, all in honour of the god in question. The most popular of these gods, the one, at least, in honour of whom the greatest number of festivals were celebrated, was Dionysus or Bacchus. He was worshipped as the god of the creative power of nature; it was he who fertilised the vines, ripened the grapes, and made the trees bud. Wine was the wealth of Greece; it was natural, therefore, that in town and country its mighty god should be worshipped in numerous festivals, either when the wine was pressed, or when it had ceased fermenting, and the first cup of the new must was to be tasted.

In his *Acharnians* Aristophanes describes the celebration of a Dionysiac feast by a peasant and his family quite by themselves. They begin with a prayer, after which the family walk in procession to the place of the offering; first comes the daughter as " Canephorus," [1] carrying the basket with the sacrifice on

---

[1] The Canephori were the maidens who at the feasts of Demeter or Dionysus were chosen to bear the baskets of sacrificial offerings.

her head, behind her the slave with a phallus, the symbol
of fertility, and finally the master of the house singing
a spicy phallic song; his wife (representing an admiring
public) follows the procession with her eyes from the
top of the house. Aristophanes meant to deride the
poverty of village festivals, which no doubt were eclipsed
by the magnificent Athenian Dionysia; but in doing so
he gives us a means of judging of the original and
plainest form of these grand celebrations. For his
simple description contains the nucleus of the Dionysia:
prayer, procession, phallic symbol, dithyramb and
sacrifice (fig. 13).

Before the Greek drama came into existence we may
imagine that the procession (the part of the Dionysia
in which we are interested) and the sacrifice may have
been celebrated somewhat in the following manner.[1]

The principal point was the *offering of the sacrifice*,
round which the other ceremonies were grouped.
Originally a human being was sacrificed, but later,
when morals improved, the man was replaced by a goat
(*tragos*). The object of the procession was to convey
the animal in a solemn manner to the place of offering.
Sometimes also the procession was combined with the
symbolic nuptial expedition which conducted the Basilinna
(wife of the Archon Basileus) to the temple where she
was to wed Dionysus. At any rate the procession was
of a purely religious character, and its members per-

---

[1] Here I take the different festivals collectively, as it would carry us too
far to enter upon the distinction between rural and urban Dionysia, between *Lenæa* and *Anthesteria*. Detailed information about this subject is
found, *e.g.*, in Paul Stengel: *Die griechischen Sakralalterthümer*. Comp.
Von Müller: *Handbuch der klassischen Alterthumswissenschaft*, Bd. v., or
Blümner: *Leben und Sitten der Griechen*, Bd. iii.

13

14

13—Ceremonies at the Feast of Dionysus.   14—Hermæ and altar of Dionysus
(from a vase).

formed an official religious mission.   One of the tasks
was to represent Dionysus himself, in case it was not
considered sufficient to carry his statue in the procession.
He was imagined—and represented—as a bearded, long-
haired, mature man[1] (fig. 14); two little horns pro-
jected from his forehead as a sign of his unconquerable
energy; in his hand he held a flourishing thyrsus, an
image of spring, and the evergreen crown of ivy which
adorned his head showed that his power of action was
not affected by the shifting season; an enormous phallus
indicative of his tremendous creative power was carried
in front of him in a basket or at the end of a stick.
Before the god marched virgins in festive attire, crowned
with garlands, bearing the basket with the sacrifice on
their slender heads, and behind him came a strange
motley group of Bacchantes fantastically arrayed as
satyrs in goatskin, or as intoxicated *Ithyphalloi* with
loose wine-stained garments, and faces smeared with
dregs or mulberry-juice, symbolical of the violent creative
power of Dionysus, and of the intoxicating, savagely
exciting influence of wine.   But according to the dogma
of his bloody death and victorious resurrection, the
god of wine was also a vanquisher of death, and therefore the dead were included in his triumphal procession.
A number of Bacchantes represented these gloomy
guests from Hades.   With white lead they imparted to
their faces a deadly pallor, or they covered them entirely
with white grave-clothes, which were afterwards thrown
aside to reveal ugly and horrifying death-masks.   These

[1] The representation of Bacchus as an effeminate youth just past boy-
hood is of later date.

members of the procession were the only ones who did not carry the official emblem, the phallus, as the dead were supposed to be sexless.

This procession, *pompê*, of satyrs, intoxicated *ithyphalloi* and *corpses* in grave-clothes, moved on to the place of offering, and here, while the animal was being prepared for the sacrifice, songs and dances were performed in honour of the god. The songs which related events of the life of Dionysus were called *dithyrambs*, and were sung to the accompaniment of flutes and dancing round the altar by the chorus of satyrs with its leader— the *Exarchon*. The popular name of a satyr was *tragos* (goat); therefore the chorus was called the tragic, or goat-chorus, and the song—tragic, or goat-song. So goat-song is the popular name of the dithyramb,[1] and what we call Greek *tragedy* is a direct outcome of the chorus. And even after the members had ceased to disguise themselves exclusively as satyrs, the popular name of *goat* or *tragic* chorus was preserved. However, the satyr chorus in its original form did not disappear, though under a somewhat different form it had become an attribute of the tragedy. It survived in the particular species of drama called satyr play; only its name was altered to *Satyrikos Choros*, the *satyric* chorus.

Thus the tragedy and the satyr play developed out of the strictly official ecclesiastical part of the Bacchus festival. By degrees, as the songs and dances of satyrs and *ithyphalloi* adopted fixed forms and rhythms, their performance claimed more special train-

[1] Baumeister: *Monuments of Classical Antiquity*, i. p. 383.

ing and particularly qualified artists. Thus the Bacchic chorus came to form a kind of staff of professional singers and dancers.

But side by side with this religious element of the festival ran a secular unofficial movement, which became the source of the merry Attic comedy. The regular Bacchantic procession of disguised figures prepared for the occasion was soon increased by a voluntary crowd of enthusiastic adorers of Dionysus and the phallic symbol; though not belonging to the official escort of the god, they were more than ordinary spectators. In a merry group (*Kômos*) they proceeded through the town, mostly on chariots, sang their songs in honour of phallus (*phallica*), and flung witticisms to the crowd, which was not loath to answer. These phallic sports were soon a standing and favourite part of the festal programme. The songs, which in the beginning were improvised, were studied by a chorus of the merry young men, which was called the *comic* chorus from *kômos*, the name of the strolling troop, and their songs were called Κωμῳδία—comedies.

Originally the members of the chorus appeared in their ordinary dress; afterwards they adopted a kind of uniform consisting of a woollen tunic and a coarse mantle made of hides sown together. They wore no masks, but their heads were crowned with ivy and violets, and bunches of thyme and acanthus leaves hung down over their heads, hiding their faces. They also carried a phallus,[1] either

---

[1] In this case, however, phallus was not, as in the *ithyphalloi*, a symbol of the creative power of Dionysus, and therefore a religious emblem, but rather a kind of amulet for protection against witchcraft, etc. Phallic figures are still used in this way in southern Europe, being placed above doors, round the necks of little children, on tombs, etc. See Ed. du Méril, *op. cit.* i.

tied to their belt or suspended from their neck.   On this account they were called *phallophoroi* (phallus-wearers).

Tragedy and *Comedy* — the two popular names of the serious and the merry play—were preserved throughout antiquity, and resumed afterwards, at the time of the Renaissance, almost with the same meaning.   As we see, both names originated from the worship of Dionysus. But it is worth noticing that, while the tragedy and satyr play formed integral parts of divine worship, and, as such, treated—either seriously or satirically—of supernatural fates and events, which had nothing to do with real life, the comedy, to begin with, was nothing but a merry improvised encounter of wit between secular attendants at the festival, the object of which was to hit each other's weak points, without any one's appearing offended, however deeply a wound might smart. This essential difference between the two forms of dramatic art was still maintained as time went on, and tragedy continued to represent the lives of gods and heroes, while comedy went on chastising contemporary follies and events of everyday life.   In what manner and through how long a period the dithyramb of the satyrs and the phallic jokes of the young men's chorus developed into what we are now accustomed to consider as a drama, is still and will most likely for ever remain unknown, so long as we are unacquainted with the transitional forms which must necessarily have existed.

The chief features of this transforming process are : first, the abandonment of the exclusively satyric character of the chorus, which has something to do with the fact that the dithyramb is no longer occupied merely with Dionysus, but also sings the lives and feats of other heroes; secondly, the transition of the head singer from being the epic interpreter of somebody else's adventures to being himself the impersonator of some hero, whose sufferings he represents as if felt by himself; thirdly, the introduction of a regular plot.

The history of literature, like other history, has its myths, and one of the most deeply rooted and widely diffused is that of Thespis and his cart. Thespis, it is said, was the "inventor" of dramatic art in Greece; he travelled round the country on his famous cart, acting his tragedies. The myth is derived from Horace,[1] and, like many other myths, has some foundation, though the feature in it which impresses itself most on the memory is a fiction. The cart has to be given up, and stage histories ought long ago to have found another vignette than the fantastic toy-chariot which has hitherto been their stereotyped symbol. We know very little about Thespis, and even this is scarcely trustworthy. He lived in the sixth century B.C., and was what in those days was called a *dancer*,[2] *i.e.* he taught the Bacchic chorus, the dances and the songs, of which he himself was the composer. Of course Thespis did not "invent" either comedy or tragedy, which were the result of slow development; but he may have been the first, or one of the first, who ventured to break with tradition, by introducing new hero-legends into the Bacchic dithyrambs, even going as far as to introduce these heroes

---

[1] *Ars poetica*, 275-77.
[2] ὀρχηστής; comp. Alb. Müller: *Lehrbuch der griechischen Bühnenalterhümer*, p. 220.

personally as living and speaking, a reform which in the beginning did not please the old Athenians—(about the year 535 Thespis, who was born in the country,[1] and mostly appeared at rural Dionysiac celebrations, brought his tragedies to Athens)—because they thought it almost blasphemous to see the old heroes represented in bodily shape, and speaking words which they had perhaps never spoken.   But the younger generation and the public at large were delighted with this method of acting, and Thespis soon found many imitators, who appeared at all the Dionysiac feasts, and courted public favour with their tragedies.

The invention of the mask is also associated with the name of Thespis; but we dare not leave him in sole possession of this honour either.   In the chapter on primitive dramatic art we have seen that even among very undeveloped peoples the mask was used as a means of mystification at religious dances, and it is scarcely probable that in the time of Thespis the Greeks were unacquainted with it, as they used other kinds of disguise and mummery.   But it is quite possible, as the reports state, that he introduced new masks, and especially that the idea of changing masks according to the persons represented was due to him.   Tradition attributes to him the use of three different disguises of the face: one consisted of a layer of white lead, the second of a similar covering of purslane, the third of a mask of delicately painted linen.

What the figures were like which Thespis represented under these masks we cannot imagine, as no remains

[1] In Icaria, not far from Marathon.

15—Sophocles.

whatever are left of his poems. Moreover, of the works of his nearest successors, Choerilus, Pratinas, and Phrynichus, almost everything is lost. Only a few scattered fragments allow us to suppose that the great name which Phrynichus acquired during his lifetime, and preserved long after his death, was not undeserved. All these men were " dancers," and all of them appeared as actors or singers in their own plays. We must not forget, however, that *there is as yet no question of a "drama" in our sense of the word.* We must imagine the Greek drama — whether tragedy or satyr play— before the time of Aeschylus, as having consisted of alternative songs between the chorus and its leader. It is only with Aeschylus that the real history of the Greek drama and Greek scenic art begins; not only because with this poet we step out of the semi-darkness of legend and conjecture into clear daylight, but especially because, under his influence, the drama, the theatre and its art, crystallise themselves into the classic forms which remain essentially unaltered throughout the whole of classical antiquity.

We do not propose to follow up the history of the Greek drama, as this task is not comprised in the plan of the present book. The history of theatrical art looks upon dramatic poetry from the point of view of *réper-toire*, and from this standpoint we will only remind our readers of some outward characteristics of Greek plays, and indicate the tasks which they imposed upon the actor.

It has been already said that on the Greek stage three kinds of dramas were enacted—the *tragedy*, the *satyr play*, and the *comedy*. Whereas from the very beginning the comedy formed a complete whole, and was performed separately, it became the custom to give the tragedy a threefold action; *i.e.* a cycle of legends was arranged into three dramas, each by itself forming a complete unity, but all being linked together by subject and chronological order, so as to form a connected work. Three tragedies thus united were called a *trilogy*. They were acted consecutively in one day, and after this substantial food the author used to serve a light dessert, the satyr play, which also presented some legendary subject, but in a merry, burlesque form.[1] Such a combination of four plays was called a *tetralogy*.

The connection between the separate pieces is only preserved in Aeschylus, of whom we still possess a whole trilogy, whereas it is observed neither in Sophocles nor in Euripides. Three tragedies are indeed acted consecutively, but the connection between them is given up, and each piece forms a complete unity by itself, independent of the other works.

However, the fundamental difference between the construction of the antique and that of the modern tragedy does not lie in the particular connection between the three or four pieces, which is explained by the circumstance that the Greeks, having no permanent

---

[1] Of all the satyr plays only a single one is preserved, *The Cyclops*, an amusing play by Euripides. It describes the visit of Ulysses to the Cyclops Polyphemus in Sicily, where Silenus and his sons (the chorus of satyrs) are kept as prisoners. It treats in bold, comical outlines Homer's story about Ulysses, who, after having made the Cyclops drunk with the wine he has brought with him, puts out his only eye, thus saving himself and his companions from death.

theatre, required longer performances than we are accustomed to see at the present time. The chief distinction is the use of the *chorus*. The tragedy, having arisen from the Bacchic chorus, retained it as its principal feature; though in the course of time its original construction was modified, so that the comic or burlesque element, which originally formed part of it, disappeared, and "tragedy" became synonymous with "serious drama."

With Aeschylus (fig. 16), in his earlier tragedies—those which appeared before the year 468 B.C., the date at which Sophocles had his first drama acted—the chorus was still the principal element; so much so, that these compositions must indeed be considered as transitional forms leading up to the real tragedy. If we read a play like *The Suppliants*, which is considered the earliest of his known works, it impresses us as being a merely embryonic drama. All the action it contains is this: the Danaides (daughters of Danaus) implore the help of the Argive king against their cousins, the Egyptiades, from whose wooing they have fled to Greece. The help is promised, and therewith the piece ends. So all the dramatic element in this and similar plays must be found in the conversations between the chorus and other persons, but the chief stress is laid on the lyric elegies of the Danaides. In Sophocles (fig. 15), the dialogue and the dramatic element are developed into real action, which, however, does not yet supersede the lyric power of the chorus and its direct interference with the course of events. But in Euripides (fig. 17), the chorus is practically superfluous; it has only to reason, and to pronounce the moral of the play as the author's mouthpiece ; it no longer acts a principal part in the tragedy, much less serves as its real basis and essential cause.

The external construction of the Greek drama further differed from ours in not being divided into acts ; the play continued without interruption to the end. Yet it consisted of principal divisions, separated by songs of the chorus. These chief parts of the dialogue, which differed much in length,[1] were called *episodes*, and resembled our acts in so far that the dialogue at their close was interrupted by music, but not so as to make a pause in the action in order to give the spectators a rest. At the same time, the Greek tragedy, especially during its earliest period, was not much longer than a long act of a modern play.

Thus most of the tragedies of Aeschylus do not consist of more than 1000-1100 lines. Sophocles is somewhat less compendious ; *Oedipus Tyrannus* is 1500 lines long, and *Oedipus Coloneus* even 1800.

As for the types which the tragedy gave the actors to represent, it must be constantly borne in mind that the serious drama, which formed part of the worship of the gods, did not occupy itself with the life and doings of human beings ; it was the grand and sad fates of gods and heroes, superhuman passions, and deep, powerful feelings, that were expressed in broad and pathetic lyric words. The object was not to reproduce in a realistic way the mental and physical life of man ; and if, nevertheless, these old poems appear genuinely human and

---

[1] In *The Persians* (Aeschylus), the first episode contains 476 lines ; the second 34 : in *Seven against Thebes*, the second episode has 349 ; the third 28 lines.

16

17

18

19

16—Æschylus.   17—Euripides.
18—Aristophanes.   19—Menander.

true to nature, they are so contrary to the intention of the author. The way of representing them (to which we shall refer further on) shows the most distinct desire to make the tragedy appear supernatural and unreal.

Comedy, as we have seen, was of less high lineage, and by its character would seem to offer richer opportunities for representation of human characters.

How the songs, dances and witty encounters of the *phallophoroi* developed into what we call Attic Comedy is a matter even less known to us than the development of tragedy. According to tradition, Greece produced 252 authors of comic plays, but of all this wealth only a few pieces of *one* single author have survived. Of the others nothing but a few fragments and quotations are left, which can only give us a very defective notion of the way in which the development took place. Still, in the Roman imitations by Plautus and Terence we possess a pretty reliable standard, by which, combined with the remaining fragments, we can form an idea of the New Attic Comedy.

Greek comedy, we know, falls into two divisions:[1] 1. the *Old Attic Comedy;* 2. the *New Attic Comedy,* which differ very much in form as well as in subject— much more, indeed, than contemporary tragedies. The flourishing period of the Old Comedy lies between the years 454 and 404 B.C., and the names by which it is distinguished are those of Cratinus, Eupolis, and, above all, Aristophanes (fig. 18). Though we are only acquainted with eleven of the forty-four pieces which Aristophanes is

[1] Several investigators, even of the most recent date, keep up the division into three periods : 1. the Oldest Comedy ; 2. the Middle Comedy ; 3. the New Attic Comedy, though it is proved that the idea of a Middle Comedy was invented by the grammarians of the time of the Emperor Hadrian.

said to have written, and with none of the other authors, we know enough to be able to see that these frolicsome old plays, the comic power of which remains, though they are several thousand years old, had a double character. They were either parodies caricaturing the same subjects that were treated seriously in the tragedy (and in this case they only differed from the satyr play in the composition of the chorus), or they took their subjects from the political, social, or literary conditions of their time ; and in the latter form they may most adequately be compared with the satirical plays, which in the most recent theatrical language are called *revues*. We must say, however, that those Greek *revues* were conceived with much more spirit and imagination, and executed with much more art and care,[1] than our own flippant ephemeral plays. They were broad satires on generally known persons and circumstances, which in the most burlesque and fantastic disguises scourged even the highest persons in the country [2] with an inconceivable boldness and wanton licentiousness. But, whether appearing as parody or as social satire, the Old Attic Comedy preserved, as a trace of its phallic origin, an unbridled obscenity in its dances, songs and dialogues. And finally, a characteristic feature of the first division of comedy is the *chorus*, which, as in the first tragedies, forms the real basis of the play, to which, also like the tragedies, it frequently lends its name.[3]

---

[1] Like all Greek plays, they were written entirely in verse.

[2] Thus *The Knights* of Aristophanes is a passionate attack on Cleon, the ruler of the state ; in *The Clouds* Socrates and other sophists, as well as their methods of education, are ridiculed.

[3] *The Knights, The Frogs, The Wasps, The Birds*, of Aristophanes.

It seems as if the taste for direct personal satire decreased, so that at last the government, without losing its popularity, was able to stop these bold attacks by law. At the same time people began to find these phallic outbursts of wit too coarse and indecent. The comedy then turned to everyday life, and chose its subjects in streets, lanes and home circles, creating universal comic types without aiming at particular persons of distinction. But in order to impart to these ordinary characters an interest which they did not possess in themselves if compared with the bold political caricatures, the authors had to place them in situations which helped to set off their follies. In this way the New Attic Comedy arose; it became a mixed drama.

This comedy flourished at the time of Alexander the Great and his successors, and is especially connected with the names of Philemon (361-262) and Menander (*c.* 342-291) (fig. 19), both of whom served as models to Plautus and Terence.

The point of these pieces lay especially in the comic power of the situations, which were always fresh inventions, not in any social satire, or in profoundly studied and original characters. The persons recur in one comedy after another, and become stereotyped characters. The most important of these are the *old fathers*, of which there are two principal types, the *irascible* and the *good-natured;* the *light-minded,* and the *honest son;* the *cunning servant;* the *greedy parasite;* the *swaggering soldier;* the *dishonest matchmaker;* the *obliging companion;* the *parasitic relatives,* and the *impudent prostitutes.*

While the chorus plays a principal part in the older comedy, of which it was the origin, it is omitted altogether from the later comedy. The new times and political conditions taxed the citizens so heavily that they could not afford to fit out expensive choruses; besides, what business had the fantastic old phallic singers in a tame domestic comedy? The new comic play sought a kind of compensation in the *prologue* (which, by - the - bye, had already been used in the tragedies of Euripides) and in the *epilogue*. As an introduction to the play, and in order to rouse the attention of the public, to impose silence and to secure correct understanding, the author made a *prologus*—as a rule a supernatural mythical being, as, *e.g.*, Zeus, sometimes an allegorical figure as *Air* or *Help*—come forward and explain the subject of the piece. After the performance the author appeared in person before the public with a collecting-box in his hand, and in an epilogue solicited approval for himself and his play. In this way he had an opportunity of speaking out his mind directly to the public, whereas the old comic authors used the chorus as mouthpiece. The Greek prologue and epilogue have frequently been imitated by later dramatists, for instance by Shakespeare. However, these forms are likewise found in mediæval and Asiatic plays, where we cannot suppose any imitation of Greek customs to have taken place. Thus it seems that this immediate appeal of the author to his public, in order to offer explanation and to ask for approval, is the outcome of a universal tendency which prevails in all times and in all countries.

II

THE THEATRE

Old and New Theories about the Construction of the Greek Theatre—Stage
or no Stage—The Stage of the Earliest Times—Theatrical Conditions
at the Time of the Classical Drama—Machinery and Decorations—
The Permanent Stone Theatre of Later Times.

THE study of the Greek theatre has shared the fate of
certain old pictures. Eager to complete, improve and
enrich the original simple outline of the subject, the
changing times have added one layer of colour on the
top of another, corrected a stroke here and added a
detail there, and at last daubed the somewhat doubtful
result with a brilliant varnish of learned argumentation.
The task of the latest investigation is, not to continue
this kind of restoration, but, on the contrary, to dissolve
the varnish, peel off the false colours, and leave nothing
but that which can be proved by evidence to belong to
the old pictures.   Let it then be incomplete, let the outlines be partly obliterated, the colours faded : it has the
invaluable advantage of being authentic.

The restored picture of the Greek Theatre, which
for so many centuries had been considered the only
genuine one, in the course of time had become loaded
with absurdities.   The classical scholars, by whom
the question of the theatre is constantly treated with
especial interest, heaped conjecture on conjecture, and
their imagination, which was more influenced by the
sight of the modern theatrical technique that was always
before their eyes than by a comparative study of the

scenic phenomena of primitive civilisation, invented even more fantastic modes of representation for the simple antique Greek drama.   We need only peruse some of the modern historians and interpreters of the classical drama to see to what degree their opinions were influenced by purely modern notions; so much so, that they attribute to the Greeks, five centuries before Christ, such mechanical masterpieces and such skill in decorative painting as were not only quite unknown in those times, but would even oblige modern engineers to strike work. Each new interpreter seemed to consider it his task to find out a new scenic absurdity to add to those of his predecessors, and all postulates were wrapt up in a tissue of quotations and comments, which at any rate made it a very troublesome work to penetrate to the real substance.

Then suddenly, not more than twelve years ago,[1] a learned investigator conceived a doubt which made the whole elaborate edifice, the construction of which had been the work of centuries, collapse no less rapidly than did the palaces on the stage imagined by more ancient scholars.

There was one feature which all conjectures and explanations had hitherto treated as an incontrovertible and uncontested fact, viz., that in the Greek, as well as in the Roman and in our modern theatre, the real action of the play was represented on an *elevated* stage, while the chorus performed its songs and dances in the *Orchêstra*, a place *especially appropriated to the purpose*.   From the sources whence this fact was derived, we learned that the stage was not less than ten and not more than twelve feet high, so that the chorus and the actors were

[1] The Danish original of this volume was published in 1897.

separated from each other by this distance. All who are
acquainted with the Greek drama know how indissolubly
close is the connection between the players and the
chorus, how their dialogues are going on constantly,
how the chorus frequently bars the way of one of the
principal persons, how they go out and come in together,
take things from each other, touch each other, etc., etc.
These facts, which are obvious enough from the dramas
—tragedies as well as comedies—had been hitherto
either explained away or left unheeded, as nobody ever
thought of doubting that the actors really performed on
an elevated stage, and the chorus in the low *orchêstra*.
Attempts were made to get over the difficulties by
admitting that on certain occasions the chorus might
mount on to the stage, while the actor was supposed
never to appear in the *orchêstra*.   Thus, at the dramatic
moment, when the tyrant was to be prevented from
committing a cruel murder, the chorus—or at least its
leader—had to climb up a ladder ten feet high in order
to step into the way of the sublime ruler.   Such and
many similar absurdities now strike everybody, but a
few years ago nobody noticed them.

Only when the German, J. Höpken, the above-
mentioned expert, expressed the doubt [1] whether the
actors and the chorus performed in separate places,
and whether it was not more likely that they acted
together in the *orchêstra*, people began to pay attention
to the innumerable inconsistencies between the statements found in the authentic dramas and the hitherto
accepted scenic arrangement.   At the same time

[1] *De theatro attico saeculi a Chr. quinti.*   Bonn, 1884.

Höpken proposed some hypothetical theories, built on the dramas, about the arrangement of the stage in the *orchêstra*; but these theories were not tenable, nor was his method. But his general view and his doubt were soon after confirmed in the most striking way.

At the instigation of the German Archæological Institute the architect, Wilhelm Dörpfeld, soon after undertook a series of excavations of Greek theatres; and these excavations, which were carried on with the greatest accuracy and sagacity, proved by evidence that Höpken was right, in so far as he doubted that plays had ever been acted on an elevated stage; for the ruins, even the oldest, did not reveal the slightest trace of such an arrangement, and the whole construction of the buildings showed clearly that the *orchêstra* must have been the common stage, where chorus and actors appeared together on the same level.

It was only by slow degrees that the learned world acquired knowledge of the results and opinions of Dörpfeld, which touched on many other questions relating to the theatre, and for one thing proved, what had been overlooked hitherto, that the large Greek stone theatres dated only from the fourth century B.C., and consequently did not exist at the time of the classical drama. In letters to other learned men, in periodicals and reviews, he indicated his discoveries, and these communications called forth a regular storm in the world of classical scholarship.

The last ten years have brought forth a deluge of

articles—professional works and large monographs [1]—in which the fight about the stage has raged uninterruptedly, and in which piles of proofs, *pro* and *con*, have been heaped up, and a whole scale of diverse hypotheses suggested. However, Dörpfeld's own principal work,[2] which did not appear till October 1896, forced his adversaries to lay down their arms, and fixed the construction and the way of using the Greek theatre.

It will be asked how it is possible for a dispute to arise about such an important question between testimonies drawn from remaining fragments of buildings and authentic dramas on the one side, and proofs derived from old critical authors, grammarians and scholiasts on the other. The answer is simple. Of contemporary descriptions of Greek theatres there are absolutely none. So students had to be contented with statements of much later authors about theatres which they had never seen, as they were all rebuilt during the time of the Romans. One of the most important and most-quoted authorities is Vitruvius. This author, who pretends to have lived under Augustus, really belongs— as has been proved by J. L. Ussing—to a period several centuries later, and his representation of ancient archi-

---

[1] Dörpfeld's chief adversaries were : Alb. Müller (*Lehrbuch der griech. Alterthümer*), Haigh (*The Attic Theatre*), Oehmichen (*Bühnenwesen der Griechen u. Römer*) ; and quite recently : E. Bethe (*Prolegomena zur Geschichte des Theaters im Alterth.*). His adherents : Von Wilamowitz-Möllendorf (*Die Bühne des Aischylos*, etc.), Capp (*Vitruvius and the Greek Stage*, etc.), Kawerau (in Baumeister's *Denkmäler*, Art. *Theater-gebände*); and in Denmark : J. L. Ussing (*Lecture at the Meeting of Northern Philologists*, 1892).

[2] *Das griechische Theater, Beiträge zur Geschichte des Dionysos-Theaters in Athen und anderer griechisher Theater;* von Wilhelm Dörpfeld und Emil Reisch. Athens and Leipzig, 1896.

tecture is, it seems, borrowed from Varro. His description of the Roman theatre agrees fairly well with the
ruins of the theatres ; but when, in speaking of the Greek
theatre, he places the stage ten to twelve feet higher
than the auditorium, he makes a mistake. His authority
had mentioned the *proscenium*, by which—according to
Greek conception—is meant the colonnade in front of
the *skênê*,[1] which, indeed, generally has this height,
but Vitruvius took the word in its Roman sense, meaning
the place in front of the *skênê* or stage.

Other principal authorities are the Greek grammarians
Pollux and Suidas, who lived in the second and the
eleventh centuries of our era respectively. Considering
that we, in our time, and with the scientific resources we
possess, had, till very few years ago, quite erroneous
ideas about our own mediæval theatre, and that these
notions keep haunting even our very latest stage-
histories, we cannot wonder in the least that a Greek
author — at a time when historical research stood on
a very low level—could not obtain accurate information
about the appearance of the theatre in his native
country many centuries before he lived.

If we are to form an idea of the old Greek theatre,
the first thing we must do is to throw overboard all
preconceived, and especially all modern notions.
Though the Greek theatre was the fundamental type of
modern playhouses, the development has been so long,
and the alterations from the original way of using it
are so great, that scarcely any common features remain.
The names, too, of the most important parts of play-

[1] House or tent at the back of the stage.

houses are borrowed from the Greek, but have nevertheless undergone the law of change, and have now a
meaning quite different from the original one.

In the beginning the Greek word *theatron* only
signified "all the spectators," "the assembled spectators"; afterwards it came to mean the space, the
place occupied by the spectators, the "auditorium," and
finally, though late, its sense was altered so as to signify
the whole building in which plays were acted. *Orchestra*,
by which we understand the place occupied by the
musicians, or in a wider sense, the band of musicians
itself, among the Greeks meant the place where the
dancing—*i.e.* the acting—was performed; for the Greek
"dance" not only meant the branch of art which we call
by that name, but mimic-dramatic representation generally. So the *orchêstra* became the *stage*. The space
itself on which the performance had taken place preserved its name, even when it had ceased to be used as
a stage; for instance, among the Romans, where a part of
it was taken up by seats for spectators, thus corresponding to what in our theatrical language goes by the name
of "pit" and "stalls." In France, as we know, most of the
places on the floor are called *l'orchestre*, *fauteuils* or
stalles d'orchestre, while we (Danes) and several
other nations have borrowed the old French name
parquet. And finally: *skênê*, Lat. *scena*, was not
what we understand by *scene*. *Skênê* means a house
built of wood or cloth, intended for a temporary
dwelling, much the same as what we call a "tent." In
theatrical language it came to mean the building in
which the actors waited when they were not performing,

in which they changed their costumes, and where in later times they also resided. How it was afterwards made to form a decorative part of the stage, we shall describe later. Here we will only explain once for all that *skênê* means the "house of the actors" and not the "stage."

As already stated, the ruins of theatres hardly give any direct information about theatrical conditions before the fourth century. So we scarcely know anything *positive* about scenic arrangements during the whole classical period, the fifth century, the time of all the great poets we admire, in short, of the whole dramatic literature with which we are acquainted; still less, of course, about the sixth century, of the literature of which only scanty fragments are preserved. But we can draw the *negative* conclusion that, as solid buildings of stone were not erected in those centuries, they must have been built temporarily of wood; and as there is every reason to suppose, judging from the generally conservative character of the performances, that the stone theatres did not differ *essentially* from the earlier structures, we are still capable of forming an idea of those structures, especially if we refer to the indications found in the dramas themselves.

As the plays were sacred performances which belonged to the worship of Dionysus, they were acted on the sacred territory near his temple; and as the offering of the sacrifice formed the introduction of the festivity, the *sacrificial altar* naturally became the centre of the representation. This altar consisted of an offering-table and an adjoining platform, on which the sacrificer stood. Fig. 20 shows such a sacrificial altar. It is an altar of Aphrodite, as there does not exist any altar of Dionysus of so early a time. The platform was called *thymelê*, a name which, by-the-bye, was also used for the whole altar.[1]

It was round this altar, on the bare ground, that the chorus of Bacchus performed its dances. In order to render the ground more fit to be danced upon, it was stamped hard and even, and the outline of the circle was marked by a circle of limestone, which formed a kind of terrace round the dancing-place, yet on the same level as the surrounding ground. This circular place with the altar as centre was called the *orchêstra*, and here we have the original plan of the Greek theatre. The circular form of the stage, of course, originated in the cyclic character of the dances, and was never altered so long as the Greek theatre existed as an independent institution.

The spectators who wished to see the dances and hear the songs of the fantastic satyric chorus—and who did not?—naturally pushed their way from all sides, only held back by the limestone border round the *orchêstra*. For these festivals it was the custom to choose places surrounded by hills or mountain slopes, which allowed the more distant spectators to overlook the dancing-place. And gradually, as the demand for comfort increased and the festivals lasted longer, scaffoldings with wooden benches were erected on the slopes and round the dancing-place, so that the public

---

[1] As to the signification of the word *thymelê* (from θύειν, to sacrifice), opinions differ very much indeed. Comp. among others : Wieseler, *Ueber die Thymelê*. Du Méril: *Le Thymélé* (La com. i., App. VI.). Müller: *Bühnenalterthümer*, pp. 129 ff. Haigh: *Att. theatre*, pp. 132 f. ; Oehmichen, *Bühnenvesen*, p. 442. Dörpfeld and Reisch : *Das griech. Theater*, pp. 278 ff.

might comfortably and without fatigue follow the sacred performance from beginning to end. When the *orchêstra* was placed terrace-wise on a mountain slope, of course these scaffoldings could not close round it; the part that sloped downward had to be left free. This was the case in Athens.[1] The poet, reciter or actor, whoever alternately with the chorus recited the hero-legends, stood at the altar in the middle of the circle, probably on the raised platform, the *thymelê*, where also the flute player, who accompanied the dances and songs of the chorus on his instrument, had his place. From this elevated point the poet was able to overlook and control the whole chorus, and, if necessary, lead its movements, for it was he who originally was its teacher, practised the performances with it, and composed all its dances and songs. The reserved seats were at first limited to the smallest possible number, so that only the most distinguished persons—the priests, the rulers of the people, and other dignitaries—had real wooden benches to sit on, whereas the ordinary man had to place himself as best he could on the mountain slope, lying down, sitting or standing, as he pleased.

The sixth century B.C. did not advance further than to this simple arrangement: a circular dancing-place of firmly stamped ground surrounded by a border of masonry, and with an altar in its centre, and an auditorium consisting of a number of circular rows of benches built of wood, and only made for each particular festal occasion. To this very day similar dances are

---

[1] Athens had two such stages, one near the Agora and one near the Acropolis.

performed on religious holidays among Greek country people. "The best male and female dancers in the village never tire of performing their circular dances accompanied by songs and simple music. It is true, we no longer see an altar raised in the dancing-place, but the musicians are still placed in the middle of it, forming a centre, round which the dancers move in a circle. Most of the spectators stand up all round ; for the most privileged among them chairs are procured and placed in the front row. A few of the spectators also find suitable seats in higher places, on terraces belonging to houses, on rocks, or even in the trees." [1]

The fifth century, which was so wonderfully productive of dramatic literature, as a matter of course also brought enlargements and novelties within the domain of the theatre. The crowding of people at the performances kept increasing, and the wooden scaffoldings soon proved insufficient, though they were constantly enlarged. It happened at a dramatic performance in Athens, where the three dramatists, Pratinas, Choerilus and Aeschylus were competing, that the scaffoldings on which the spectators were seated, collapsed, and caused a dreadful accident. Therefore, in order to avoid similar misfortunes, it was an urgent necessity first of all to enlarge the auditorium and render it more solid. This was done by adapting the ground on which the auditorium was placed, so that the scaffoldings became superfluous ; the benches were placed on the earth or on the rocks, always in circular rows surrounding the *orchêstra*, and always of

[1] Dörpfeld: *Das griech. Theater*, pp. 368 f.

wood.   Of stone benches of the fifth century no traces whatever have been found in Greece.

The stage, on the other hand, preserved its old simple form of a circular dancing-place with the altar in the middle of it, and the plays conformed their requirements to this simplicity, which indeed has great advantages. The *orchêstra*, we may say, was the bottom of a funnel formed by the auditorium, and there the actors and the chorus moved about, mingling with one another just as in a modern circus-pantomime the *corps de ballet* and the principal persons act together in the ring.   All the spectators in the rows of the amphitheatre had an equally free view of the performance on the stage, which would by no means have been the case if the actors had performed on an elevated platform in the background. Such a raised platform, as Dörpfeld justly observes, is only necessary where the spectators are sitting or standing on the same horizontal level.   Where the spectators are seated on an ascending slope, an elevated stage is decidedly less suitable than a low one.   The annexed drawings will show this distinctly.   In fig. 21*a* the actor is on the same level as the spectators, who are seated on an even plane, and the lines of vision of the spectators seated behind each other coincide, so that indeed the foremost only has a full view of the performers.   Fig. 21*b* shows how the spectators on a gradually ascending slope all have an equally good view of the actor; whereas it becomes clear from fig. 21*c* that an actor standing on a high "stage" is partly concealed from the eyes of the nearest spectators, if he does not keep quite close to the edge of his elevated platform.

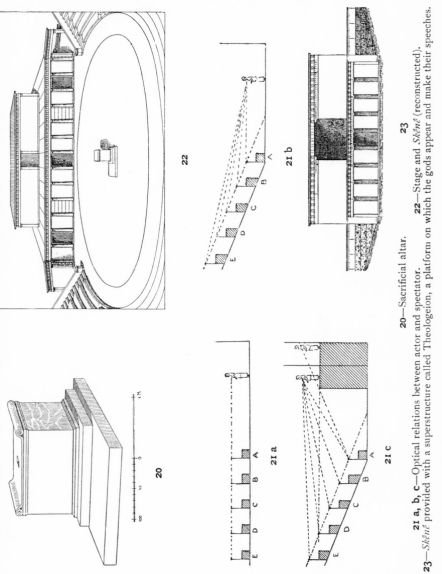

20—Sacrificial altar.

21 a, b, c—Optical relations between actor and spectator.

22—Stage and spectator.

23—Skênê (reconstructed). 22—Stage and Skênê (reconstructed). 23—Skênê provided with a superstructure called Theologeion, a platform on which the gods appear and make their speeches.

This arrangement also seems to have been best from the acoustic point of view. From what we have said it becomes evident that the stage as well as the auditorium was uncovered, but, in spite of this, words spoken from the orchestra in the immense ruins of ancient theatres are heard most distinctly even in the remotest seats.

The scenic arrangement, then, of the old Greek theatre was very different from that of later times, and naturally its means of working were also very different. While our modern stage tries to represent as in a frame true pictures of life, assisted by realistic, illusory, decorative painting, effects of light, invisible machinery, curtains which fall and rise between the changing tableaux, etc., the aim of the Greek stage lay in a very different sphere. Perhaps we might say that, if our theatrical art is *picturesque*, ancient Greek dramatic art was *plastic*. The persons who appeared on the orchestra might be looked upon from all sides like statues; they produced an independent personal effect, and did not enter like figures in a picture. No landscape or other background helped them to conjure up certain localities before the eyes of the spectators; they entered on the stage, which was nothing but a bare platform, and thence they worked by their words and tones. During the first period of the Greek drama no attempt was made to give an illusory image of life, but exclusively to tune the mind to devotional compassion for the sufferings of the great heroes, or, as in the old comedy, to change this feeling into its opposite through a fantastic parodic representation. Therefore in the Greek theatre of the classic age we never find a direct imitation of nature; everything—

costumes, masks, elocution and movements—is fantastic
or conventional. We cannot point out sharply enough
this absolute difference between the ancient Greek
and our modern theatre; and we may suppose that, if
it had been constantly kept in view, people would not
have taken so much trouble to invent the multitude
of untrustworthy and sometimes quite absurd details
of scenic arrangement, which have so long distorted
and confused the picture of the ancient Hellenic
stage. As a fact it never—at least never in the most
ancient times—represented any particular place: it was
the stage whence the words of the poet were spoken, but
it did not show the *image* of the place he described, any
more than a lecture hall changes according to the poems
declaimed by a reciter, or than a concert hall illustrates
the music which is performed in it.

Nevertheless, the poet made use of existing material
to assist the representation. Originally this material
consisted only of the altar as the centre of the
orchêstra. This altar was drawn into the action, but
always on the understanding that it was a permanent
fixture in the same place. However, it was not always
made to represent an altar; in the *Prometheus
Bound*, for instance, it figures as the rock to which
Hephaestus ties the revolting god. But the surrounding space constantly remains without any defined
character. Now the play mentions the trackless
desert,[1] to which Hephaestus, accompanied by Strength
and Force, has brought Prometheus; now it is the air in

---

[1] "To earliest remotest plain we now are come
To Scythia's confine, an untrodden waste."—vv. I, 2.

which the Oceanides (the chorus) fly ; [1] now an undetermined space in which Hermes appears.   And the
scene is for the most part undetermined, if it does not
change in a quite fantastic way, as in most of the
comedies of Aristophanes, which for this reason afford
the best proof of the fact that, even at so comparatively
late a period as the time of the Aristophanic comedy, no
attempt was made to give the stage the illusory appearance required by each situation.   For, if the author
were to be followed on his fantastic flight, the demands
which these comedies make in the way of scene-shifting
would take away the breath of every modern engineer,
much more of the ancient, who, not to speak of
defective technical resources, had to work in the open
air by daylight, and, so to say, before the eyes of
the spectators.   Thus we remind our readers of *The
Peace*, in which play we are first taken to a place
which must be supposed to be a kind of pig-sty, where
the gigantic beetle of Trygaeus is fed, whereupon the
said Trygaeus mounts on the beetle and flies up into the
air.   Now for some time the scene is laid partly on
earth near the house of Trygaeus, partly in the air, till at
last the beetle mounts right up to heaven to the palace of
Zeus.   Thence, without any pause in the action, we are
again taken down to the earth.   In the introduction to
the Danish translation of the play, N. V. Dorph [2] offers
an explanation of this scenic trick, which is typical of the
way in which earlier times transferred modern theatrical

[1] " Fear not ! a friendly troop we reach,
   On rival-speeding wings this cliff forlorn."
                    (Miss Swanwick's translation.)
[2] Danish philologist, 1783-1858.

conditions to these old works.   He writes : " The illusion of this ascent was produced in this way : the surrounding stage gradually sank into the earth (!) or floor, and the palace of the god was let down slowly instead, upon which Trygaeus dismounted from the beetle and found himself in front of the abode of Zeus. . . . At the close of the first part Trygaeus and his companions disappear by back—or side—stairs, and when during the *parabasis* the previous appearance of the stage has been restored, he reappears on it, as if he had descended from above (! ?) "   Nothing can be plainer ! Only, this kind of scene-shifting, had it been practicable —which it certainly was not—in the open theatre, where all ropes, etc., would have been seen, could not have produced the slightest illusion.   We shall explain on a later page how things of this kind were carried out ; but that no local illusion was aimed at, is made evident by the same play.

Trygaeus, on coming down from heaven with Opora and Theoria, takes leave of the chorus, which consequently must be supposed to be in the same place as he, and it sings :—

"Go then, and joy be with you—we meanwhile
To our attendants give the charge to guard
This furniture, since many thieves are wont
About the scenes to lurk, as criminals.
But guard these manfully—while we declare
To the spectators all our reasoning mind."

(Wheelwright.)

So without scruple the illusion is broken, and the stage is simply mentioned as what it is.   But nowhere is it consistently spoken of as the particular locality in which the action is supposed to take place. We frequently read the expressions : "here," "hither," "here where we are sitting," etc., without more precise indication ; they mean here on the stage, and nowhere else. This same phenomenon, that the action is supposed to take place only on "the stage," and not in any defined locality, is very frequent in theatres which lack decorative pictorial development. We have seen how the Indian drama abounds in words meant to unfold ever new fantastic images before the spectators, and how far it was from making the actual stage follow suit. The wealth of picturesque words stands in inverse ratio to the poverty of resources by which the stage in itself can create illusion ; the expert playwright does not picture in many superfluous words what the spectator can take in by a glance.[1]

However, as stated above, the author, of course, profits by what is at hand ; and thus, even in the oldest known drama by Aeschylus, the altar is drawn into the action by way of illusion. In reading *The Suppliants* it at once becomes clear that the altar is the centre of the whole action. It is decorated with images of the gods, and with green branches ; steps lead up to it, and it must have been high and solid. The Danaides are grouped round it, old Danaus is seated at the foot of it,[2] the king is looking up to it with

---

[1] Strange to say, this point of view has never been expounded in the comments on the way in which Greek theatres were used. Even Dörpfeld, and especially his co-operator, Reisch, are still on a few points blinded by modern associations.

[2] *Chorus* : " Beside thee now my seat I fain would take ! "—V. 198.

veneration, and finally the maidens threaten to hang themselves on it in despair if the king does not promise them his help.   In a similar way the altar is made use of in most of the classical dramas ; without, as has been observed, necessarily representing an altar, it always serves as a fixed point of support, as some object which not too unreasonably might be supposed to resemble it in shape.   In *The Persians* it is the sepulchral monument of Darius ; in *Prometheus* a lonely projecting rock.[1]   But nothing justifies us in believing or even in supposing that, under such circumstances, the altar was transformed in a particular way, or that a real monument or artificial rock was built for each of these respective purposes.   Why should not the spectator's imagination fancy an altar to be a rock as easily as it made the flat dancing-place represent now a holy grove, now a seashore, or innumerable other things ?

However, when Sophocles appears, we meet in his dramas, as well as in the later ones of Aeschylus, with a new fixed point of support for the action.   Whereas Aeschylus, in his earlier dramas, never alludes to anything stationary but the frequently mentioned altar, it is evident that Sophocles, who in more than one respect was a reformer, nearly always presupposes a *building*, out of which his persons come, into which they retire, in front of which the action takes place, the doors of

---

[1] *Hephaestus* : ". . . But I of daring lack, a brother god
Fast to this storm-vex'd cleft perforce to bind."

Prometheus : ". . . Behold and see
In what dire bonds unenvied watch I keep,
Clasp'd to the summit of this rock-bound steep."

which are opened, etc. Simultaneously this building appears in those of the tragedies of Aeschylus—*e.g.*, the *Oresteia* — which were acted after the appearance of Sophocles. As a rule it is imagined as a palace, sometimes as something else, but always as a kind of house or dwelling; thus in the *Philoctetes* it represents a cave with two entrances, in the *Ajax*, a tent. It also happens that in one and the same play it represents first one locality, then another.[1]

The addition of this *building* to the stage apparatus originated as follows.

So long as the chorus consisted exclusively of satyrs, were so dressed, and came to the place of festival in procession, while the actor was only a narrator, no changes of costume were needed, and consequently no dressing-room. But afterwards, when actors as well as chorus appeared now in one costume, now in another, *e.g.*, either as young maidens or as young men, it became necessary to provide a room where dresses and masks might be changed unseen by the spectators. For this purpose a house or tent, the *skêne*, was built, to which the players retired on leaving the stage. In the beginning this house was probably situated at a considerable distance from the *orchêstra*, and out of sight of the spectators; but it soon became necessary to bring the *skêne* much nearer, so that now, as the number of persons in the drama went on increasing, the actors might change their dresses without delay. And then it was that an ingenious dramatist, probably Sophocles,

[1] For instance, in the *Acharnians* of Aristophanes.

conceived the idea of joining the *skênê* to the stage and giving it importance in the play.[1]

However, in order that the *skênê* might be worthy of forming a portion of the festal domain, it had to appear in a decent shape, and could not remain merely a modest wooden shed. So a kind of decorative façade was built in front of the dressing apartment, a row of wooden pillars, the intervals between which were filled with planks, canvas, rugs and hides. This decorative wall was called the *proskênion*, the front wall of the *skênê*, and it was erected quite near the circumference of the *orchêstra*, which it generally touched. So this façade and the adjoining *skênê* cut away part of the auditorium, which had previously formed almost a perfect circle round the *orchêstra*. Between the *skênê* and the auditorium were two entrances, one on each side, by which the spectators entered the theatre, and the chorus came on the stage. The actors also made use of these side entrances called *parodoi*, if they were not supposed to come out of the building. In this case, which was the most frequent after the *skênê* had been introduced as a point of support in the action of the play, they entered through (one or several) doors, which were inserted in the façade for this purpose. This decorative wall, the *proskênion*, was not stationary; it was removed after the close of the festivities, whereas the *skênê* (fig. 22), which also served as store-

[1] We feel quite sure that Dörpfeld is mistaken in his opinion (*Das griech. Theater*, p. 370), that the dramas necessitated a decorative background. Here, as everywhere, the expert dramatist adapts himself to the given conditions of the stage in all important matters, and the scenic conditions do not change in order to conform themselves to each special drama.

room for masks and other properties, etc.—later even as a residence for actors—remained in its place.

The *proskênion* was ten to twelve feet high ; the *skênê* was of the same height, or had sometimes two storeys.   Its roof was flat, and where the *skênê* was in two storeys, the roof of the *proskênion* formed a kind of terrace, to which the upper storey of the *skênê* served as background.   In that case this storey had also a large door leading out on the above-mentioned terrace.

Aristotle states quite briefly in his *Poetics*[1] that Sophocles introduced *skenography*, viz., the art of painting or decorating the *skênê*.   Aristotle was not grown up till about half a century after the death of Sophocles, and his statement does not give any absolute certainty beyond the fact that there existed something called skenography.   Meanwhile this short remark has been interpreted and extended to the effect that Sophocles introduced painted back-cloths on the stage ; and in all works about the Greek theatre we find detailed descriptions of the way in which they were arranged, and of what they represented in the different cases.   It is to be supposed that the authors of these works, in this case also, made the mistake of applying modern scenic conditions to the ancient stage without considering the difficulties of such conclusions.   We cannot see, indeed, why the remark of Aristotle need mean anything but that Sophocles introduced the custom of decorating the background of the stage, the wall called the *proskênion*, which stood in front of the building, serving as *skênê* or store-room, and made this wall

[1] *Poetics*, iv.

form part of the stage.   About the *way* in which he had
it decorated, we know nothing.   During this period the
proskênion was built of wood ; so it was natural that,
in order to produce an impression of beauty, harmonising
with the magnificent many-coloured dresses, it should
have been painted in an artistic way.   That these
paintings, however, were of a merely architectural
character, we may conclude from the fact that most
of the plays allude to some palace, temple or house, and
that if, as an exception, they refer to a cave or a tent,
the same background with its architectural decoration
served to represent such localities : nobody is likely to
have thought of expecting a realistic representation of
a grotto, or the like, such kind of representation being
altogether out of the question.

To these two objects, the altar and the decorated
wall, we must consider the permanent decoration of the
stage as limited, so far as the classic age is concerned,
viz., the fifth and the beginning of the fourth centuries.

If we are to give a brief statement of the appearance
of the theatre at this period, we may describe it in the
following way : a circular stage, the *orchêstra*, on which
chorus and actors appear together ; in the middle of the
stage an altar ; surrounding the stage for more than
half of its circumference the auditorium (or *theatron*),
which consisted of wooden benches in broad rows gently
sloping upward ; on the opposite side, the circle round
the *orchêstra* closed by the *skênê* and the decorated
wall in front of it, the *proskênion* ; between the *skênê* and
the auditorium, which are not achitecturally connected,
we find an entrance—*parodos*—on each side, through

which the spectators have access to their seats, and the chorus—sometimes also the actors—to the *orchêstra*.

We have still to mention some scenic peculiarities of the classical time, which come in under the name of what we call *machinery*. Unfortunately the surviving dramas do not give any direct information as to the nature of these phenomena in the domain of machinery, and the earlier, but not contemporary authors, such as the above-mentioned Pollux, have only been able to form a somewhat confused idea of them. No wonder then that this branch of theatrical technique has been a good battle-field for the most hazardous and complicated conjectures of scholars, and that within the four walls of learning the different tricks of stage-technique have shaped themselves into the most fantastic forms. We cannot say that the excavations of later years and the more rational conception of theatrical phenomena, which was a consequence of them, have brought to light real positive facts respecting the nature of Greek machinery; still, the hypotheses can now be kept within reasonable limits, and though the results cannot be considered as finally proved, at least they appear plausible, even to a merely practical eye.

Every one knows the expression *deus ex machinâ*, and is aware that it means the god who, at the close of the piece, by his supernatural appearance, solves the highly complicated plot. Nor is this dramatic contrivance in itself unknown in modern plays. If at the most critical point of *Tartuffe* the police officer unmasks the hypocrite, and by royal dictate returns the lost property to the dupes, we say that he acts as a *deus ex machinâ*.

But what the machine was like on which the god made his appearance, and whence the expression and the idea originated, are questions which those who are otherwise familiar with the saying have probably never explained to themselves.

In the earlier period of the Greek drama, far from being unusual, it was a customary theatrical convention that the gods should walk among the heroes of the plays, so there was no reason to use particular means for distinguishing the appearance of the gods from that of the other characters. People were not afraid of seeing Hermes and Athenê with the same aspect and on the same level as Ajax and Orestes, appearing in the orchestra with their fellow-actors.[1] But as early as the time of Euripides this condition of things and this way of viewing the gods were changed.

In the Euripidean drama we are further removed from the naïve intercourse of gods and men, which belongs to the popular *epos*. Here the god is imagined as a sublime being, different from man, and ruling over him, and the natural consequence of this conception is, that the scenic appearance of the gods becomes different. As Euripides was the inventor of the dramatic trick of making a god appear at the critical moment and solve the difficulty by an imperative sentence,[2] where the plot was so tightly complicated, that a natural solution seemed impossible, he was probably also the inventor of the scenic apparatus which carried out his idea.

[1] Comp., *e.g.*, *The Eumenides, Ajax.*
[2] For which he is scoffed at by Plato as well as by the comedian Antiphanes.

We have mentioned above that the actors sometimes talked from the roof of the *proskênion*, and nothing prevents us from supposing that the gods frequently made their appearance there, simply stepping forth from the upper storey of the edifice, which had an opening in front (comp. fig. 23) ; but this simple arrangement was not always practicable. Thus in the *Orestes* of Euripides it is distinctly indicated that Apollo is soaring with Helena in the air above the roof of the palace (*proskênion*) on which Orestes, Pylades and Hermione find themselves,[1] and that he flies away at last to the "star-covered" vault, carrying off Helena to the festal hall of Zeus. In *The Mad Hercules* Iris and Lyssa (the goddess of insanity) appear in a similar way in the air above the roof, and while Iris flies away, Lyssa descends into the dwelling of Hercules (down behind the *proskênion*) in order to derange the hero's mind.[2]

Both passages furnish good examples of the manner in which a "god from the machine" acted in tragedy. But in some parodic comedies by Aristophanes we find even a better illustration of the actual technical contrivance, and they expressly confirm what the whole nature of the theatre justified us in supposing,

---

[1] "Here can I see her now high in the vault of heaven," v. 1631.

[2] "Ay, and I soon will dance the madder, and pipe thee quite out of thy mind with fear !

So, up with the famous foot, thou Iris, march to Olympos, leave me here,

Me and mine, who now combine, in the dreadful shape no mortal sees,

And now are about to pass, from without, inside of the home of Herakles."

In *Aristophanes' Apology*.   Robt. Browning.

viz., that the whole apparatus was not very illusive in its effect, but, on the contrary, made a ludicrous impression on critical minds, especially when taken in connection with the whole of the *mise-en-scène*, which was anything but realistic.

In *The Clouds* of Aristophanes we know that Socrates appears in the air like a god, and from this height he addresses himself to Strepsiades, who, miserable inhabitant of the earth, finds himself in the *orchêstra*. The following conversation takes place :—

Strepsiades. Hoa! Socrates. What hoa, my little
              Socrates !

Socrates. Mortal, how now! Thou insect of a day,
              What would'st thou ?

Str. I would know what thou art doing.

Soc. I tread in air, contemplating the sun.

Str. Ah! then, I see you're basketed[1] so high,
           That you look down upon the gods — good
              hope,
           You'll lower a peg on earth.

Soc. Sublime in air,
           Sublime in thought I carry my mind with me,
           In cogitations all assimilated
           To the pure atmosphere in which I float ;
           Lower me to earth, and my mind's subtle powers
           Seiz'd by contagious dulness, lose their spirit ;
           For the dry earth drinks up the generous sap,
           The vegetating vigour of philosophy,
           And leaves it a mere husk.
                        (Mitchell.)

---

[1] ἀπὸ ταρροῦ (v. 226) ταρρὸς, wicker basket, net-work.

From what follows it is clear that Socrates is let down on to the *orchêstra*, where the conversation is continued.

So this machine for the gods was evidently an apparatus of net, or other plaited work, in which the flying person was suspended. The rope which held the apparatus cannot reasonably have been fastened anywhere but on the roof of the *skênê*; whence, it is supposed, by the help of a crane—such a machine is expressly mentioned by the ancient authors—the actor was lifted up, let down, or turned away, and made to disappear behind the back wall of the *skênê*, as the case might be. How this crane was applied, and how the machine was constructed in its details, is not easy to understand, and will scarcely ever be explained. That Socrates is suspended in a kind of basket or hammock seems to indicate that the gods, when appearing in serious plays, used a similar apparatus, a net or coat of mail, such as are also used by modern engineers for flying figures, in order to keep the body erect and to divide the pressure. Aristophanes, in his parody, may have converted this machine into one of wickerwork, perhaps resembling those which were used in everyday life for drying figs.

In *The Peace* we meet with another comical use of the flying machine of tragedy. We have elsewhere mentioned the passage in the comedy of Aristophanes where Trygaeus ascends to heaven on his beetle. This little scene a parody on the famous aeronautic excursion of Bellerophon, treated by Euripides : the beetle takes the place of the winged

Pegasus, with which Trygaeus compares it when setting out on his ride.

> " But on, my Pegasus, proceed with joy,
>   Exciting with the golden-bitted reins
>   A sound agreeable to thy glad ears."
>
> (Wheelwright.)

These lines were perhaps a direct quotation from the Euripidean tragedy, and so the whole situation would work on the initiated spectator with doubly comical effect, seeing that the outward apparatus was also an imitation of the tragic model.   Now we see Trygaeus mount on his beetle in front of his house (viz., the *skênê*).   His goal is heaven, the dwelling-place of Zeus.   Now it ascends, and, sitting on his "winged foal," as he calls it, Trygaeus remains a good while in the air, all the time expressing his fear to the audience that the beetle, following its natural tendency, may throw off its rider and seek its food in a dung-hill.

> " What doest thou ? what doest thou ? where bend
>   Thy nostrils ? to the filthy lanes ? transport
>   Thyself from earth with confidence—and then
>   Unfurling thy swift wing, with course direct,
>   Pass onward to the halls of Jupiter.
>   Keeping thy nose removed from excrement
>   And all ephemeral food."

At last the timid Heaven-seeker reaches the palace of Zeus.

> " But methinks
>   I'm near the gods and view th' abode of Jove.
>   Who is the porter there ?   Will you not open ? "
>
> (Wheelwright.)

Then Hermes comes out from the dwelling of Zeus, and the action goes on between those two on the roof, while the other persons act "yonder below,"[1] viz., in the *orchêstra*, till finally Trygaeus has to leave heaven, and says :—

Trygaeus. O beetle, homeward, homeward let us fly.
Hermes. He is not here, O friend.
Try.   Then whither gone ?
Her. Following Jove's car he bears the thunderbolts.
   .   .   .   .
Try. How then shall I come down ?
Her.   Courage ! quite well
      Here by the goddess' self.
                           (Wheelwright.)

After which Trygaeus leaves the stage till, after a while, he reappears "on earth," *i.e.* in the *orchêstra*.

With our present knowledge of the arrangement of the Greek theatre we have no great difficulty in imagining the acting of this scene in its principal features. The beetle was a variety of the flying apparatus which, as we have seen, was used by the gods in the tragedy. In the beginning the flying beetle was placed in the *orchêstra*, while its strings went up into the crane fixed in the roof of the *proskênion*. Here he alighted, and this roof now represented the court in front of the palace of Zeus, whence afterwards Trygaeus again descended to the *orchêstra*; in other words, here—as often elsewhere — the *skênê* had a second storey, with a door opening on the platform of the *proskênion*

---

[1] Comp. v. 224, *Try.* "In which (cave) ?"—*Her.* "The one yonder below." V. 313, "Beware of him down yonder . . ."

and with stairs leading down to the lower storey, from which, of course, there was access to the *orchêstra*.

It was formerly thought that the *machine for the gods*, the *flying machine* and the *crane* were three different scenic apparatuses, each serving its particular purpose and having its particular structure. However, it seems more natural to suppose that the three contrivances, the name of which we know chiefly from authors who did not understand their use, were one and the same machine, only appearing under different names; and that this machine was indeed the above-mentioned flying machine which we have just attempted to explain.

There is another machine, however, which cannot be classed under the same heading. It goes by the name of *ekkyklêma*, and though in modern times attempts have been made to deny its existence, though there is more confusion concerning its actual construction and the manner of using it than there is about the flying machine, there cannot—it seems—be any doubt that this peculiar apparatus was really employed.

Here, too, the parody is even more instructive than the serious representation itself, and we must again refer to the comedies of Aristophanes, in order to obtain the true image through its caricature.

In *The Acharnians* Dicaeopolis goes to the house of Euripides to borrow a tragic costume. Euripides, however, is just composing poetry, and does not want to come out of his house. So Dicaeopolis knocks at his door, and the following dialogue ensues between Euripides inside, viz., behind the *proskênion*, and Dicaeopolis outside, viz., in the *orchêstra*.

D. Euripides! Euripides, come down,
    If ever you came down in all your life!
    'Tis I, 'tis Dicaeopolis from Chollidae.

E. I'm not at leisure to come down.

D.   Perhaps—
    But here's the scene-shifter can wheel you round.[1]

E. It cannot be.

D.   But, however, notwithstanding.

E. Well, there, then, I'm wheel'd round,[2] for I had
       not time
    For coming down.

                               (Frere.)

So Euripides is "wheeled round," and—as we gather from the subsequent conversation — appears in a reclining attitude[3] surrounded by the costumes of his most pitiable heroes, and among these he makes his servants choose one for Dicaeopolis.

In the *Thesmophoriazusai*[4] a similar scene occurs. Here it is Euripides and his old brother-in-law Mnesilochus who apply to Agathon, the tragedian, to borrow a woman's costume, under which disguise Mnesilochus is to steal into the assembly of married women. Agathon, like his colleague in *The Acharnians*, is absorbed in his poetry, and is "wheeled round" in the like manner, surrounded by his attributes.[5]

---

[1] ἀλλ' ἐκκυκλήθητι.—Arist. *Acharn.* v. 408.

[2] ἀλλ' ἐκκυκλήσομαι.—*Ibid.* v. 409.

[3] ἀναβάδην.—This expression has always been translated by "high up," but Reisch (*Das griech. Th.*, p. 238) very appropriately remarks that this interpretation is improbable.

[4] "The women celebrating a festival." Thesmophoriæ were the festivals held by married women in Athens in honour of Demeter.

[5] Comp. Arist. *Thesmoph.*, v. 95, 96, 239 and 265.

In both these cases the parodic representation of the *ekkyklêma* is used satirically against tragic authors, and shows us that it was a peculiarity of theirs—not exactly approved of—to represent in sight of the spectators things which really ought to be hidden from them. If we compare some passages in the tragedy, where the *ekkyklêma* must indeed be supposed to have been used with these two parodies, we obtain a pretty clear idea of its proper function.

In *The Mad Hercules* the chorus finds itself alone on the stage, while Hercules in his castle is attacked by the goddess of insanity, and kills his own children in his rage; the chorus is ignorant of what has happened till a messenger relates it; but after the news has been delivered, Hercules appears before the eyes of the chorus —and of the spectators—as he lies after his furious rage, asleep and bound, near the dead bodies of his sons. The chorus says:—

> " Woe ! woe ! behold !
> The portaled palace lies unrolled,
> This way and that way, each prodigious fold !
> Alas for me ! these children, see,
> Stretched, hapless group, before their father—he
> The all-unhappy, who lies sleeping out
> The murder of his sons, a dreadful sleep !
> And bonds, see, all about—
> Rope-tangle, ties and tether—these
> Tightenings around the body of Herakles
> To the stone columns of the house made fast ! " [1]

(Browning).

[1] Euripides : *The Mad Hercules*, v. 1028-1041.

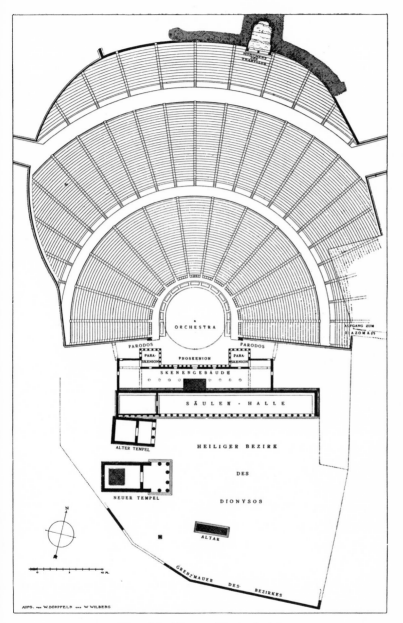

MONUMENT DES THRASYLLOS

ORCHESTRA

AUFGANG ZUM PLAZOMA(?)

PARODOS   PARODOS

PARA-   PROSKENION   PARA-
SKENION   SKENION

SKENENGEBÄUDE

SÄULEN - HALLE

ALTER TEMPEL

HEILIGER BEZIRK

DES

NEUER TEMPEL

DIONYSOS

N

ALTAR

GRENZMAUER DES BEZIRKES

AUFG. von W. DÖRPFELD und W. WILBERG

24—Plan of the Dionysus Theatre in Athens.

At the close of the *Antigone* Creon is informed by
his servant in a similar way of the death of his wife.
The servant says to his master, who is bemoaning his
son, having carried his corpse on to the stage on his
arms :—

> My lord and master! Thou art master here
> Of nought but sorrows. One within thine
> arms
> Thou bring'st with thee, and in thy palace
> halls
> Thou hast possession of another grief,
> Which thou wilt soon behold.
>
> *Cr.*   What more of woe,
> Or what more woeful sounds anew from thee?
>
> *2nd M.* The honoured mother of that corse, the
> queen,
> Is dead and bleeding with a new-given
> wound.
>
> *Cr.* O! O! O!
> O charnel gulf of Hades, choked with dead,
> Why harrowest thou my soul?
> Ill-boding harbinger of woe, what word
> Didst utter? Oh thou has killed me o'er
> again,
> Before undone! What say'st? What are
> thy news?
> Ah me!
> A slaughtered wife thrown on the pile of
> ruin?

Here we must suppose that the dead body of

Eurydice is wheeled on to the stage, for the messenger replies :—

"No longer hidden in the house.   Behold."

Similar examples can be drawn from all three parts of the *Oresteia* of Aeschylus, from the *Ajax* of Sophocles, in which the inside of this hero's tent is represented, from the *Hippolytus* of Euripides, and from the *Electra* of Sophocles.   As a rule, it is the dead body of some one who has committed suicide, or of one who has been killed off the stage, which is represented in this manner ; sometimes, as in the *Ajax*, living persons are brought forward on the *ekkyklêma* ; sometimes, as in the *Eumenides*[1] and in *The Mad Hercules*, it brings whole groups of sleeping or dead persons on the stage.

The tragedies by themselves do not show distinctly that such a machine was really wheeled forward from the *proskênion* to the *orchêstra*, bearing the figures supposed to come out from inside the building.   They only state that the doors open and the figures appear. It has in fact been doubted that such was the case, and it has been suggested that the decorative back wall was divided, each part being pulled aside in order to present the new scene to the spectators ; however, it seems evident from the two parodic comedies (from their words as well as from their sense) that a machine was used. What could be the object of parodying such a simple thing as the opening of doors to reveal an *intérieur* to the audience ?   If it was deemed preferable to have a machine wheeled into the *orchêstra* rather than to

[1] The last tragedy of the *Oresteia*, the trilogy of Aeschylus.

25—The Dionysus theatre in Athens (present state).

arrange the groups inside the *proskênion*, no doubt it was owing to the circumstance that a very large part of the audience would have been all but excluded from seeing the events presented inside.

About the construction of the *ekkyklêma*, however, we cannot say anything definite. It was most likely a simple platform—higher or lower, as the case might be —resting on cylinders or wheels, which was moved on to the *orchêstra* and held by ropes, by which it could be pulled back again behind the *proskênion*.

A frequent means of effect, in comedy as well as tragedy, was the *thundering machine*, which consisted of hides inflated and filled with stones, which were beaten against metal plates.

In some Greek ruins there have been found beneath the central part of the *orchêstra* entire caves,[1] which, if not obviously serving other purposes, are supposed to have been used like the modern traps, from which the spirits of the dead made their ascent. If this explanation holds good, we feel sure that the so-called *Charonic ladders* were used here, as, according to the latest interpreters, they were made precisely for this purpose.

We may add, finally, that in the dramas the characters are frequently described as entering in chariots, and that this was really so is beyond doubt. The side entrances and the *orchêstra* gave room enough, and it was quite in harmony with the general character of the

---

[1] In Eretria, for instance, is found a subterranean passage which leads from the interval between the *proskênion* and the *skênê* to the middle of the *orchêstra*, and which has a flight of stairs on each side.

plays to introduce such kind of realism as consisted in processions and festive pomp.

But from everything which, in the modern theatre, is understood by *effects of light*, the Greek stage, of course, was entirely debarred. The open, uncovered stage and the view of the surrounding landscape would at any moment even belie the words of the play. While in the mouth of the tragedian the storm was howling, the tempest raging, the lightning flashing through the air, the spectators saw a serene azure-blue sky above their heads, and while the hero followed the march of the stars on the nocturnal heavens, the sun darted its scorching rays down on the top of his head. It has been said indeed that night was sometimes represented by black draperies ;[1] but, of course, this can only have been the case when the play was acted on what we call a covered stage. On the whole, the ancient Greeks required no more illusion of time than of locality.

The drama of the fifth and the first part of the fourth centuries, the beauty and noble forms of which precisely suited the national taste, developed a passion for theatrical representation, which found expression among other things in the massive and magnificent playhouses, the ruins of which, diffused all over Greece and its colonies, still call forth our admiration and excite our curiosity. Whereas the drama itself never afterwards had a flourishing period which could be even approximately compared to that of the fifth century, but on the contrary deteriorated by degrees, the demands with regard to its outward frame constantly increased and produced

[1] Comp. Oehmichen : *Bühnenwesen*, p. 240.

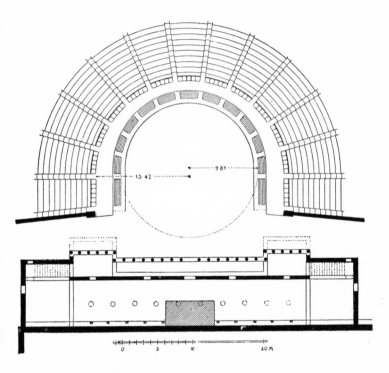

26—Normal plan of a Greek theatre.

colossal architectonic enterprises, not only in the capitals, but also in towns of secondary rank, which must have incurred considerable pecuniary sacrifices to satisfy the people in its craving for theatrical entertainment. It is not known for certain at what time the first stone theatre was built in Greece. In Athens the theatre of Dionysus, in its stone form, was constructed between the years 350 and 325, and it was finished by Lycurgus (fig. 24), but it is not certain that this theatre was the first in Greece. On the other hand, no ruins have as yet been found dating from an earlier period than this. It may be considered, then, as pretty certain that the latter half of the fourth century marks the period when stone theatres were introduced.

In their construction and use these theatres only differ from the previous wooden buildings in the solidity of their material. They too were divided into three different portions :

A. The Auditorium (*Theatron*),
B. The Stage (*Orchêstra*),
C. The Playhouse (*Skênê*).

The form and size of the auditorium vary considerably in the different theatres, but the general outline was always nearly semi-circular, without being entirely confined to this shape. It was only in the Roman theatre that the audience was placed in regular semi-circles. As in former times it was still preferred to build the auditorium where nature came to the assistance of the architect, viz., on gently sloping hillsides (fig. 25). Where support was required, solid walls were erected to prevent the earth from slipping, and stone seats were carved in the rocks where the natural condition of the ground allowed it. The auditorium was divided lengthwise by one or two passages (*diazomata*) running all round from right to left, and crosswise by radiating flights of stairs, dividing the tiers of seats into a kind of boxes, *kerkides*. Of course these passages and stairs were made to facilitate access to the places (comp. fig. 26).

As to the seats themselves, which were called *hedolia*, their shape was peculiar and fairly practical, but not very comfortable. There was no back to them, and the spectators had to sit on the stone steps; but in order to give more room, and to prevent people from being kicked by those who sat behind them, the steps were divided into two parts, a higher one in front serving as seat, and a lower one at the back on which the persons on the seat above rested their feet. Moreover, the seats were hollowed out so as to allow the person seated to draw in his feet under the seat (comp. figs. 27 and 28), which left more room for the passers-by. By these means the further advantage was obtained of accommodating the largest possible number of spectators within the smallest space. There was no further division of the places, and they were not numbered. As a rule these hard stone seats were covered with cushions, which, however, were brought by the spectators themselves. The front row, which contained the seats of honour set apart for a few persons of particular distinction, was separated by a narrow passage from the ordinary tiers, which, with true democratic uniformity, were exactly alike in appearance. In this foremost row we find the priest

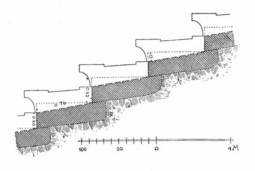

27

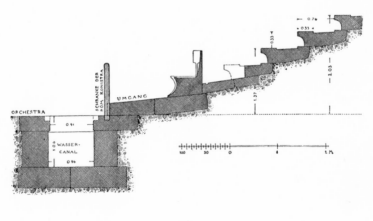

28

27—Profile outline of the seats.   28—Section of the spectators' seats.

of Dionysus (in the middle), foreign ambassadors, generals, archons, benefactors of the State, the children of heroes fallen in battle, all of them seated in beautifully carved marble chairs, which—more comfortable than the other seats—were provided with high backs (comp. figs. 28 and 30). Originally admission to the performance was free of charge. Afterwards, when the management of the theatres passed into the hands of lessees who rented them, the audience had to pay for seats. Pericles, however, had a law passed which ordained that this expense should be defrayed by the State. The price of admission for one day of performance was two obols (ab. 3d.), for the three-day festival of the great Dionysia, one drachma (about 9¾d.). This was the price for all places in the theatre except the seats of honour. The tickets (fig. 29), of which a number still exist, all dating from the time of the Roman Empire, were either small leaden marks half the size of a farthing, or somewhat larger ivory disks. On their surface some sign was engraved, such as a mask, a theatre, a bust, sometimes also the title of the piece or the name of the author. Besides this mark the ivory ticket showed the *kerkis* (wedge) or box to which it gave admission. The leaden marks, which had no such sign, must be supposed to have given admission to the auditorium in general, whereas the ivory tickets indicated the specially reserved seats.

The number of seats for the audience varied immensely in the different theatres. The latest authorities do not give the colossal figures of earlier ones. Thus Dörpfeld estimates that the theatre of Dionysus at

Athens was capable of containing 17,000 spectators, while formerly it was supposed to have had room for more than 27,000. The theatre of Megalopolis was the largest in Greece, and, according to Dörpfeld, could contain 20,000 persons, according to earlier calculations 44,000. The theatre in Ephesus is even supposed to have been large enough to accommodate 50,000 people.

It is further stated that a row of *sound-basins* were put up in the auditorium with the purpose of increasing the resonance of the voices of actors and chorus. Vitruvius, one of the earliest writers about the Greek theatre, even mentions a whole system of differently tuned basins, each of which, when its particular tone was spoken or sung, was put in vibration, thus increasing the strength of the tone. But how these basins were placed, we cannot make out from this description. In a few ruins of theatres niches have been discovered, of the purpose of which no better explanation could be found than that the above-mentioned sound-basins may have been placed in them.

As the performances always took place by broad daylight, of course there was no artificial light; the climate also allowed the auditorium to be uncovered (fig. 32). Broad-brimmed hats were worn as a protection against the sun. The awning (*velarium*) was not introduced till the Roman period.

The *orchêstra* underwent scarcely any changes during the new period. It continued to be a circular place of firm ground with a spot for the altar in the centre. In the stone theatres, however, a canal of masonry was built round the place for the rain to run off by. Sometimes

29

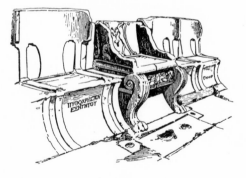

30

29—Play tickets.   30—Places of honour in the theatre of Dionysus.

little stone bridges led across the canal from the auditorium to the *orchêstra*.[1]

But the *skênê*, instead of being a temporary wooden house, became a portly stone building, not commanding in height, but fine and solidly built. Two projecting wings, the *paraskenia* (comp. figs. 24 and 26), one on each side of the façade, completed the *proskênion*, which in the fourth century was still movable, and consisted of wooden pillars, with decorated "flats" (*pinakes*) fixed between them, which might be removed and shifted according to the requirement of each play. It is not till a later date, the third and second centuries, that we meet with *proskênia* consisting of a colonnade, between the pillars of which also movable *pinakes* could be applied.

The *skênê* and the *proskênion* were about twelve feet high, which was the usual height of ordinary Greek houses; but in most theatres a second storey was added, which, however—at least as late as the fourth century—was still built of wood. This second storey was used in the same way as in the classical period. On the whole, the outward forms and conditions of acting in the later period were precisely the same as before, and it does not even seem that this period acquired a greater variety of means of creating illusion than those which we know to have existed in the fifth century. On the contrary, the fact that the *proskênion* was fixed and consisted of stone pillars, excluded the possibility of any essential variety of background decoration; while at the

---

[1] This arrangement, however, which was introduced in the theatre of Dionysus at Athens, was soon given up as impracticable. The theatre in Epidaurus, which in many respects was a model building, had only a low stone-covered water-pipe with subterranean outlet (comp. fig. 31).

same time the old repertoire, which might often be *supposed* to require different decorations, was constantly performed, though it was partly superseded by the sober spirit of the later comedy, where the scene is always laid in the *street*, or rather in some undefined place between the dwellings of the principal persons.   As a background to this comedy the later Greek fixed *skênê* with its colonnade in front and its different—generally three—doors leading into it was most suitable.   Each of the doors might perfectly well pass for a separate house, and the *orchêstra* was always there as the undefined abstract stage outside these houses.

The transition from this simple Greek scenic arrangement to the Roman construction with its elevated stage, approaching the modern structure, and the natural adaptation of the latter to the varying requirements of the times, will be described more in detail in the following section, which deals with the Roman drama.

III

THE CHORUS

THE performers in the Greek dramas were divided into three rather sharply defined classes : (1) *chorus ;* (2) *actors ;* and (3) "*supers.*"   Among these the members of the chorus were originally the only performers,

31—Theatre in Epidaurus.

whereas actors and "supers" were only added afterwards. It has been ascertained how the share of the
chorus in the tragedy gradually decreased, and in the
works which still exist we can follow this decrease in a
tangible way from the first dramas of Aeschylus to
the last of Euripides. Thus, in *The Suppliants*, the
earliest tragedy of Aeschylus, the songs and speeches
of the chorus form altogether about three - fifths of
the whole piece, in his later works scarcely one-half.
In Sophocles its share is considerably reduced, the
proportion here varying between one-fourth and one-
seventh of the whole tragedy, and in a few tragedies of
Euripides it falls as low as one-ninth.[1]

But at the same time its importance also is reduced. In *The Suppliants* the chorus is the principal
character, whose fate forms the centre of the whole
action ; the other characters are only accessories. But
gradually the tables turn. Even in *Prometheus*, we
feel more attracted by the speeches of the actors than
by the songs of the chorus, and in Euripides the chorus
is merely accessory, while all interest centres in the
actors. Agathon, the tragic author, went still further ;
in his pieces the chorus had nothing whatever to do
with the play itself ; its songs and dances were only interludes, which might even be transferred from one tragedy to
the other, thus only serving to interrupt the action, and
to give the actors and the public the necessary rest.

We are incapable of pursuing the history of the
chorus in the comedy, as we are only well acquainted
with one comic author, but we may be sure that the

[1] Comp. Haigh : *The Attic Theatre*, pp. 259 f.

development was the same.   Even in *Plutus*,[1] the last comedy by Aristophanes, the part of the chorus is reduced to a minimum, and in the New Comedy it has entirely disappeared.

Thus, while the literary history of the chorus shows a constant decline, its external construction and appearance are more durable.

To procure, equip, and train a dramatic chorus was a duty, a kind of tax, which was laid upon the more wealthy citizens of a town in turn.   The man who was chosen to defray the expenses for the training and dressing of the chorus was called the *choregus*, and it was he who had to bear not only the pecuniary, but also the artistic responsibility for the appearance of the chorus, as it was he also to whom—at least officially— the prize in the dramatic competition was awarded. Of course the amount of expense partly depended on the kind of piece performed, but partly and essentially on the greater or lesser extravagance of the *chorêgus*. As the representations were competitions between different authors and *chorêgi*, we frequently find a more or less noble rivalry between the latter as to who could spend most money on the equipment of the chorus ; and it occasionally happened that citizens, whose vanity was stronger than their cash-box, ruined themselves by providing their chorus with the most gorgeous garments.   Nor was this always to the advantage of good taste ; Aristotle expressly mentions it as a proof of vulgarity to equip the chorus (especially the

---

[1] After *Plutus* (388) Aristophanes had two more comedies performed, *Kokalos* and *Eolosikon*, but both of them are lost. Of *Plutus* an earlier edition of 408 was in existence, but it is no longer extant.

32—Theatre in Eretria.

comic chorus) with unnecessary splendour. On the other hand we meet with economical *chorêgi*, who hired old costumes for their people. Especially in later times, when the performances grew more frequent, this became a general custom.

But beyond choosing and paying for the costumes and procuring a locality for the training of the chorus, the *chorêgus* did not occupy himself personally with it. As it was an official and religious task to act in the scenic performances, only free citizens were allowed to be members of the chorus. But as both singing and dancing required natural ability as well as practice, a staff of men—women were never employed—soon came to be established, who were always employed in this work (fig. 33). The teaching of the parts was undertaken by a chorus-master or teacher, who was engaged and paid by the *chorêgus*, but who in the earliest times of the theatre was identical with the poet himself. Thus, among others, Phrynichus and Aeschylus are celebrated for the ingenuity which they exhibited in composing the dances of the chorus, in which they sometimes figured personally. In later times, after the classical period, when the plays were frequently written by orators and other men who had no knowledge of the stage, and who entirely lacked technical education in singing and dancing, the training of the chorus was put into the hands of professional teachers. The offices of master of the chorus, *chorodidaskalos*, and of dancing-master, *orchestrodidaskalos*, were established as permanent means of livelihood.

The old dithyrambic chorus consisted of fifty men called *choreutai*. When the custom arose of acting four plays consecutively, this large chorus was probably divided into four small ones, each consisting of twelve *choreutai*. It is a matter of fact, at any rate, that the oldest tragedy and satyric play was performed with a chorus of twelve. Afterwards—under Sophocles—the number increased to fifteen, as it was joined by a permanent leader, *Choryphaios*, who directed the movements of the chorus on the stage, and his two assistants, the *Parastatai*. The comic chorus always contained twenty-four members.

When the chorus was to appear on the stage it marched in military order from the left entrance (*i.e.* left of the audience) into the *orchêstra*. A flute-player always marched ahead playing the time, and later accompanying the songs and dances on his instrument. It was considered very important to have a clever flute-player, and the *chorêgi* plotted and conspired against each other in trying to acquire the best players.

The choruses were drawn up in ranks (στοῖχοι) or, less frequently, in files (ζυγά). The tragic chorus marched in three ranks, each consisting of five men, or in five files, each of three men ; the comic chorus in four ranks, each of six, or in six files, each of four men. The finest men were placed in the front rank, the plainer ones in the middle.[1] The leader always had his place in the centre

---

[1] Strangely enough, in the chorus of modern theatres—in operas as well as ballets—as a rule the opposite principle is followed, the members being placed according to seniority, so that the most advanced in age present themselves in the first rank, whereas the young novices, half concealed, peep out from behind their older colleagues. Everywhere these veterans strictly maintain their traditional prerogatives, and this is the reason why we can travel all over Europe, constantly wondering why the female choristers on all the great opera-stages are old and ugly.

33

34

33—Chorus-teacher at work.   **34**—Bird costumes of a play-chorus.

of the front rank, and had one of his assistants—the *parastatai*—on each side.

In order to give a clear idea of the arrangement of the chorus, we subjoin the following diagram, which shows how the tragic as well as the satyric chorus were placed:

SKÊNÊ.

ⓚ   ⓛ   ⓜ   ⓝ   ⓞ Rank 3.

ⓕ   ⓖ   ⓗ   ⓘ   ⓙ Rank 2.

ⓐ   ⓑ   ⓒ   ⓓ   ⓔ Rank 1.

File 1.   File 2.   File 3.   File 4.   File 5.

AUDITORIUM.

c is the leader, b and d the *parastatai*. When the chorus is drawn up by ranks the first rank is a, b, c, d, e. If a turn is made to the right a, f, k becomes file 1 (zygon). The second rank, f, g, h, i, j consists of the inferior members, for whether drawn up by rank or by file, they are the least noticed by the audience.

ⓢ   ⓣ   ⓤ   ⓥ   ⓧ   ⓨ Rank 4.

ⓜ   ⓝ   ⓞ   ⓟ   ⓠ   ⓡ Rank 3.

ⓖ   ⓗ   ⓘ   ⓙ   ⓚ   ⓛ Rank 2.

ⓐ   ⓑ   ⓒ   ⓓ   ⓔ   ⓕ Rank 1.

File 1.   File 2.   File 3.   File 4.   File 5.   File 6.

On arriving at the *orchêstra* the chorus occupied the

places prescribed in the play.   Sometimes at the beginning of a drama the chorus were supposed to sit at the
foot of the altar, or to be grouped in some other way.
This, however, did not prevent them from making their
entrance in the above-described way, and the piece did
not begin till the chorus had arranged itself in the
attitude required.

As a rule the performances of the chorus on the
stage consisted partly of *speech*, partly of *melo-dramatic
recitation*, partly of *singing* and, finally, of *dancing*.   The
speaking and reciting were no doubt done exclusively
by the leader, who alone had the right to speak on
behalf of the chorus.   Occasionally, however, speeches
were distributed among the *choreutai*, where the piece
prescribed that several members of the crowd, or of
whatever body they represented, were to contribute their
share to the dialogue.   About the singing we know
but little, not much more than that it was always in
unison ; polyphony was unknown in the Greek chorus.
Of course its artistic character varied very much according to the different pieces ; in tragedy, solemn
hymns or heart-rending elegies ; in the satyric play,
wanton and mocking goat-songs ; and in comedy, a
hubbub of the most grotesque and fantastic phallic
ditties.   But these choral songs always struck the key-
note of the play, thus to a certain extent making compensation for the lack of decoration and other means
of impressing the audience.   It was a favourite achievement, especially in comedy, to imitate certain natural
sounds which were connected with the character of the
chorus.   Thus in *The Clouds* of Aristophanes the

rolling of the thunder is imitated by the cloud-chorus.
In *The Birds* we find imitations of birds' songs like
the following :—

> Tiotio, tiotio, tiotinx—
> totototototototototinx—
> tiotio, tiotinx,

or the song of the hoopoe :—

> Huphup, voovoo! huphup, voovoo!
> trioto, trioto, toto brinx
> torotoro, torotoro, toro tinx—
> kikabau, kikkabau
> torotoro, torotoro, lililinx, etc.

In *The Frogs* the invisible frog - chorus sings as
burthen to its verses, while Dionysus is rowing in
Charon's boat :—

> Brekekekex, koax, koax.

In the same way Eupolis, a contemporary of Aristophanes, in his comedy *The Goats*, presents a goat-
chorus, which imitates the bleating of these animals, that
were so popular in Greece. Sometimes the choral songs
in the comedy were quite nonsensical. Thus the
Athenian Kallias wrote a drama about the alphabet,
a "grammatical play," in which the twenty-four letters of
the Ionic alphabet formed the comic chorus. Its songs
were produced in this way : all the consonants were
successively combined with each separate vowel. The
first verse of this interesting poem was as follows :—

> βῆτα ἄλφα βα, βῆτα εἶ βε
> βῆτα ἦτα βη, βῆτα ἰῶτα βι
> βῆτα οὖ βο, βῆτα ὑβυ
> βῆτα ὦ βω

In close connection with the recitation as well as with the singing was the dancing of the chorus.   The words, whether spoken or sung, were always accompanied by dancing, and the *choreutes*, who was incapable of supporting his verses by fine and expressive dancing movements, did not enjoy much consideration.   Even metrical art borrowed some of its technical terms from dancing. Thus the shortest division of a verse was called a "foot"; a verse of two feet was called *basis*, which originally meant step, pace; the expressions *arsis* and *thesis*, which in metrical art stand for the accented and unaccented divisions, were derived from the movements of lifting up and putting down the foot, a proof of the inseparable connection between verse and gesticulation. We deliberately say *gesticulation*, for Greek choral dance meant more than what is now understood by dancing, viz., chiefly movements with the legs.   So in translating the Greek word *orchêsis* by "dance," its meaning is not exhausted, as it also denotes the rhythmic, descriptive and symbolic gesticulations of arms, head or body, by which the chorus illustrated the words of the drama.   This kind of "dancing" was carried to a very high degree of perfection during the period when the poets themselves were "dancers," who instructed their choruses in person and invented their movements.   The *choreutai* could not add expression to their speech by facial play, as their heads were always covered by masks; it was natural therefore that they should try to render their gestures as expressive and picturesque as possible.   A complete technical system of gesticulation was composed, which afterwards in the Roman pantomimes was established as an independent artistic speciality. But by degrees as the part of the chorus was thrust more into the background, and as the poets ceased to be scenic officials, capable of teaching in person these rhythmic gestures, the art languished ; and even as early as the close of the fifth century B.C. the comic poet, Plato, complains of the deterioration of the plastic achievements of the chorus. " In the old days," he said, "a dancer was a sight worth seeing, but the *choreutai* of the present day stand in a row like so many cripples and bawl out their songs without any attempt at appropriate motions and gestures." [1] The chorus also performed real and very complicated dances. The figures of these dances were composed by the poet, and were called *schêmata* ; if presenting special difficulties, they were marked — in the same way as our present ballets—with chalk lines on the floor of the *orchêstra*. The great tragic poet Sophocles, who had to give up acting on account of his weak voice, was an excellent dancer, and did not disdain to appear as a performer in the dances he had composed for one of his own tragedies.

Each of the three different species of drama possessed its characteristic dance. That of tragedy was solemn, measured, majestic and stately. It was called *emmeleia*, and must probably be imagined as a kind of procession or march with grave, mournful gestures, which varied according to the situations required in the play. The conclusion of the *Persians* of Aeschylus gives an idea of what this dance was like.

[1] Haigh : *The Attic Theatre*, p. 287.

Xerxes desires the chorus to share his grief at the defeat they had suffered, and exclaims :—

X.   Weep, weep our loss, and to the palace go.

Ch. Alas! Alas! Woe! Woe!

X.   Responsive cries intone.

Ch. An ill bequest of ill to ill.

X.   Wail forth thy cadence shrill.

Ch. Woe! Woe! Alas! Woe! Woe!

X.   Heavy, in sooth, the blow,

Ch. Which sorely I bemoan.

X.   Ply, ply, the stroke, lift for my sake your cries.

Ch. Woe fraught, I weep amain.

X.   Wail with responsive groan.

Ch. This case, my liege, I own.

X.   Swell loud the doleful strain.

Ch. Woe! Woe! Alas! Woe! Woe!

X.   Mingled with many a blow!

Ch. Yea, black, and fraught with sighs.

X.   Ay, beat thy breast and raise the Mysian wail.

Ch. Pain, grievous pain!

X.   And from thy chin pluck out the silver hair.

Ch. Woe-fraught we pluck amain.

X.   Rend with shrill cries the air.

Ch. Cries shall not fail.

X.   With forceful hand tear thou thy bosom's stole.

Ch. Pain, grievous pain!

X.   Our host lamenting rend thy tresses too.

Ch. Woe-fraught me rend amain.

X.   Let tears thine eyes bedew.

Ch. Tears downward roll.

X.   Wail forth responsive cries.

Ch. Alas! Alas! Woe! Woe!

X. Now to thy home with cries of sorrow wend.

Ch. Alas! with wailing Persia's land resounds.

X. Through Susa let your moans ascend.

Ch. I moan, yea, moan amain.

X. Slowly advancing pour your sighs.

Ch. Alas! with wailing Persia's land resounds.

X. For those who perished in our triremes, woe!

Ch. Thee I'll escort with piteous notes of pain.

(Anna Swanwick.)

In these doleful cries, with their ever-recurring monotonous verses, we seem to see the rhythmic movements of the chorus, interrupted by the postures its members had to assume to obey the order of the actor—for instance, "Ay, beat thy breast and raise the Mysian wail," or in symbolising it (*e.g.*, "let tears thine eyes bedew"—"tears downward roll"); for in the latter case the streaming of tears could only be expressed by gestures—the face mask, remaining immovable, could not assist in expressing changes of feeling. And with solemn dancing steps the old Persians finally leave the stage with Xerxes.

Diametrically opposed to the *emmeleia* was the wild, licentious *kordax*[1] of comedy, the horror of all decent people on account of its coarseness and lasciviousness. Even Aristophanes, who inserted it in several of his other pieces, and who on the whole cannot be accused of prudery, boasts in *The Clouds*[2] that in this comedy, intended for a refined audience, he does not resort to the *kordax* or to other phallic vulgarities. Another

[1] Comp. p. 11. [2] V. 540.

piece of his gives us a sufficiently distinct idea of its unrestrained character, even if we do not see where its gross immorality comes in.   In the final chorus of *The Wasps* we read :—

Semichorus I.

O children of illustrious line,
 Whose sire is lord o'er Ocean's wave,
Approach, your sportive choirs entwine
 Where fruitless sand the waters lave.
Brothers of shrimps in circling dance,
 Your feet with Phrynic [1] lightness move ;
And one among your train advance,
 Bearing his lofty heels above,
That the spectators may the view
 With shouts of wondering joy pursue.

Semichorus to Philocleon.

Twin round in circles, and thy stomach beat,
Cast your legs heavenward, and like tops become—
For the great sire, who rules the sea, comes near,
Pleas'd with his triple row of dancing sons.
But if you love the dance, lead us out quickly,
For no one has before accomplished this,
A comic chorus capering to dismiss.

(Wheelwright.)

The *sikinnis* of the satyric play was a kind of parody on the tragic *emmeleia*, and is reported to have been very grotesque and violent in its movements.   The dancing *choreutes* in fig. 35 gives us an idea of this kind of dance.

---

[1] Phrynichus, the poet, was famous for his agility in dancing.

35—Choreutæ and actors

rformance of a satyric play.

The costumes of the choruses varied very much, and were adapted to the nature of the play in which they appeared, and to the persons they were to characterise. On the whole, in contrast with the costumes of the actors, a certain realism was aimed at, which was otherwise alien to the Greek theatre. Moreover, there was always this consideration—that they had to allow of free movement in dancing. Masks were always worn, but they do not seem to have been particularly adapted to each individual *choreutes* in the same piece. In fig. 35, a vase-painting from the National Museum at Naples, the chief persons and chorus of a satyric play are represented. All the *choreutai*, except the one who is dancing, carry their masks in one hand, and all of them exhibit the same bearded satyr-face with long bushy hair. Thus it was no doubt everywhere : when the chorus consisted of old men, they all appeared with the same white-bearded face ; if it represented young maidens, all of them had similar round cheeks.

In tragedy the chorus generally consisted either of old men, of women, or of young girls, who wore the usual Greek dress, a tunic and a mantle. As the persons represented were ordinary mortals, they had to appear in their customary clothes, thereby forming a contrast to the peculiar figures of the actors. If the characters impersonated were of a superior order, this was likewise shown by the costume. Even in *The Suppliants*, where the chorus consists of the daughters of Danaus returning from Egypt, allusion is made to their strange foreign dress. For *The Eumenides*, where the chorus consisted of these horrifying creatures,

Aeschylus invented a costume which afterwards became typical of these terrible goddesses of revenge. In black garments, with frightful painted masks, and with serpents plaited among their wild ringlets, this chorus rushed into the orchestra, spreading horror among the unsophisticated spectators, who had never yet seen such a display of fancy.

It was, however, in comedy that fancy exhibited its wildest extravagance. The Old Comedy, as mentioned above, was fond of using all kinds of absurd creatures in its chorus; Aristophanes has his wasps, his frogs, his birds; Eupolis his goats; and Archippus his fishes. In all these different choruses we see distinct traces of the animal dances which belong to the earliest repertoire of amusements of most peoples, and which, in ancient Greece as elsewhere, had had their ardent admirers. Of the costumes of those figures we can form an idea from the reproduction (fig. 34) of an Athenian vase-painting belonging to the first half of the fifth century, consequently as authentic as possible. Whether it is taken from a comedy or only from a mimetic dance we cannot decide; but this can be of no consequence, as undoubtedly the costumes of these performances were essentially alike. We see here two dancers, clothed in a fantastic feather dress, with burlesque masks on their heads, wings on their arms, feather combs on head and knees, their feet free, and with no more trappings than are compatible with the free movement of the body. In a similar comic conventional way we must imagine the choruses of Aristophanic and other comedies to have been attired.

In the satyric play the *choreutai* were naked, only wearing a hide round their loins, with a phallus and a tail attached to it (comp. fig. 35). Whether the nakedness was genuine or simulated by a kind of fleshings, like that of the actors in comedy, is not clear.

IV

THE ACTORS

Peculiar Position of the Actor—The Division of Actors into Three Classes, and their Relation to the State—Societies of Actors and their Salaries — Masks and Costumes — Mode of Performance and Technical Training—Importance of the Voice—Periods of Dramatic Art and Celebrated Actors.

THE Greek designation of the actor, properly speaking, was *hypokritês*.[1] With our modern notions we should not hesitate to give the name of actor to the leader of the chorus, who frequently had a great and important part to play, which was not less artistic in its character than the other parts, as well as to the artist impersonating, for instance, a messenger or similar character. Not so in Greece. Here was a sharp distinction between those who belonged to the chorus and those who performed the real characters. But this difference was entirely formal. While, as stated above, it was the business of the *chorêgus* to supply the chorus and provide for its training and equipment, it was the

---

[1] From ὑποκρίνεσθαι, to interpret or answer ; so "hypocrite" originally means one who answers the songs and speeches of the chorus, or who interprets the old legends.

state itself which engaged the actors, and only he was a *hypokritês* who had been engaged by the state. No importance whatever was attached to the artistic difference between the work of the *choreutai* and of the *hypokritês*, nor was the name of *hypokritês* applied to the "super," who, in case the number of players engaged by the state was insufficient, undertook a part in the drama. In other words, the ideas conveyed by "actor" and *hypokritês* are not quite equivalent. While by the name of actor we understand every reciting dramatic performer, the *hypokritai* only constituted a limited number of such performers.

Originally the dramas were represented by the chorus only with its leader as sole reciter. Later Thespis was credited with the important invention of adding another person who, independently of the chorus and its leader, impersonated such and such a hero, or perhaps several heroes consecutively, who, under different masks,[1] carried on the dialogue with the leader of the chorus. But even Aeschylus did not content himself with this one actor ; he added another, and finally with Sophocles the number increased to three. It is asserted that the Greeks never went beyond this number, so that all the dramas we know must have been acted by two or three actors respectively, together with the leader of the chorus, who could only perform his own part.

There is some uncertainty about this matter; and though the question has been treated frequently and most thoroughly, it does not seem to be solved yet. To begin with, the dramas generally contain more than two

[1] Comp. p. 100 ff.

36

37

36—Scene from a comedy.   37—Scene from a comedy.

or three characters; however, this difficulty might be removed by the fact that the same actor, whose identity was concealed by mask and costume, was, as time went on, made to perform several parts in one play, a proceeding which no doubt was frequently resorted to, and which might also appear natural enough if the pieces were always composed with this practical aim. But this is not so. We grant that in the plays of Aeschylus— besides the leader of the chorus—there are never more than two *speaking* persons in the same scene, and likewise in Sophocles and Euripides never more than three ; but even in *Prometheus*[1] no less than four characters are introduced at once in the first scene, one of whom (Bia) is and remains mute, whereas Prometheus himself, who keeps silent during the dialogue of Hephaestus and Kratos, begins to speak as soon as the two others have left the stage. And in several passages of the *Oedipus Coloneus* of Sophocles, four real actors are required ; nor can a still greater number of actors who sometimes appear in the comedies of Aristophanes be reasonably explained away. And several pictorial representations of dramatic situations show more than the fixed number of three persons, like the vase-paintings in figs. 36 and 37.

In order to get over the most troublesome of these stumbling-blocks, scholars have not recoiled from the most brain-racking experiments of thought, which, nevertheless, testify more to the honesty of their intention than to their experience of the stage. Thus, for instance, in *Prometheus*, they make Hephaestus and his companions enter carrying a wooden doll, which is supposed

---

[1] The tragedy of Aeschylus.

to represent the revolting god, and this doll is chained to the rock; but as soon as the others have left the stage, it is miraculously transformed into one of these same actors. Even the most tenacious interpreters have been compelled to confess that several of the inferior parts at least must have been performed by others than the three permanent actors.[1] In his great work on ancient comedy, Ed. du Méril proposes to interpret the three actors as representing three different *modes of delivery*, under which all the parts of the piece should be classed; and this explanation would be very plausible indeed, inasmuch as the character of the voice, and thereby the mode of expression, had the greatest weight in the casting of the play, were it not for the fact that all the authorities expressly mention three actors. This fact cannot be disputed.

But as it is equally impossible to declare that these three must always have been sufficient, and that there could not have been more than this number, it seems as if the whole affair must be reduced to a formal question, that of the official meaning of the word *hypokritês*. At the expense of the state three actors were assigned to each poet, and it was left to him to employ them as he pleased. If he wanted more, he had probably to provide them himself, or the *chorêgus* undertook their equipment, together with that of the chorus. Now, whether these inferior players were called *hypokritai* or not, as a matter of fact they performed the

---

[1] Comp. among others A. Müller, *op. cit.* p. 175, and the interpretation of F. L. Vibe, which, though somewhat more plausible, is quite impracticable on an *orchêstra*; preface to *Prometheus Bound*, p. 34 f. Beer: *Zahl der Schanspieler bei Aristofanes.* Leipzig, 1884.

work of actors. Thus it is and must be misleading to maintain that the Greek plays were never performed by more than three actors. To what extent the three *hypokritai*—the three official performers—as has been asserted, by means of rapid changes of costume, really performed all parts wherever it was possible, must remain an open question; there does not exist any trustworthy information on this point. But if, nevertheless, in several cases unofficial actors were employed, it would seem unreasonable to burden the *hypokritai* with troublesome and frequently hurried changes of costume in order to recite a more or less irrelevant speech, or to comply with a principle which after all was not consistently carried out. In the great majority of Greek plays the number of really prominent characters did not exceed three, and these, of course, were always assigned to the *hypokritai*, who were paid by the state; these artists no doubt also undertook to perform the few very important parts which did not belong to the above category. But it is absurd and unnecessary to suppose that the most distinguished actors were constantly rushing backwards and forwards between the stage and the dressing-room, in order to perform parts for the performance of which there was a sufficient number of inferior actors.

The most probable supposition is, that there existed a higher class of actors who were professionally trained and paid by the state, and a lower class, who perhaps were not called *hypokritai*, and were neither paid nor appointed by the state, but who were procured by the *chorêgus*, the real manager of the performance, and paid by him, if paid at all.

However this may have been, the genuine *hypokritai* were divided into three classes, according to their special abilities : the *protagonists*, the *deuteragonists*, and the *tritagonists*.   And just as the chorus, whomsoever it might represent, was only composed of men, so none but men appeared in the different parts of the plays, even if they had to represent quite young girls.

We nowhere read that the actor who had to play a female part tried to adopt the falsetto voice, as did the Chinese and Japanese actors ; nor is it probable that he would do so, considering that from the beginning but little weight was attached to such kinds of naturalistic effect in the Greek theatre, where everything was much more conventional than in our own.   It would seem natural, on the other hand, that the *timbre* and pitch of the voice should have been a concurrent motive in deciding whether an actor were qualified for the part of a protagonist or not.   Considering that part of the recitation was purely musical, and that the melodiously modulating element was evidently more prominent than in our recitation, we may perhaps conclude that the tripartition of the actors corresponded to the division of our opera singers into *tenors*, *baritones* and *basses*, so that the tenor with his clear penetrating voice became the *protagonist*, who was seconded by the soft and flexible, but less dominating *baritone* of the *deuteragonist*, whereas the sterner and graver character of the *bass* was more appropriate to the dignified parts which fell to the share of the *tritagonist*.   This interpretation is not put forward as a fact, only as a suggestion which might throw a little light on the hitherto somewhat obscure relation between the three classes of actors.

So much is certain, that the division of actors into three classes is a permanent classification, not a temporary distribution in the case of each separate play, though in so far decisive as to the rank of the actor, that the parts of the protagonist were as a rule the greatest and most important, those of the deuteragonist the secondary, and those of the tritagonist the comparatively least prominent. Otherwise it is not easy to see from the sparing information we possess about this matter what were the ruling principles in the distribution of the parts.

A very great number of female characters, *e.g.* Antigone, Medea, Clytemnestra, Electra, Merope, etc., were acted by protagonists, which also seems to indicate that the pitch of the voice had some weight in the allotment of parts. At any rate its *strength* was not decisive. Cicero reports that the deuteragonist and the tritagonist had often to subdue their voices, if they were naturally stronger than that of the protagonist, in order to allow the latter to shine the more.[1] In the Greek drama the interest was generally concentrated in one character, the central figure, who, like Prometheus, Electra or Hercules, gathered the whole action round himself or herself, leaving the others in the shade. These parts always fell to the share of the protagonist, who thus in most cases became the real sustainer of the piece. Therefore it was of the utmost importance to the poets to secure a prominent protagonist, as the

[1] Cicero : *Divinatio in Cæcilium*, § 45.

success of the drama depended essentially on him.   In
the ordinary theatrical language we read also that the
protagonist "played the piece."   When old plays, the
authors of which were dead, were revived, it was the
protagonist who distributed the parts and conducted the
rehearsals.   In new pieces, however, both these duties
devolved on the poet in so far as he was capable of pre-
siding over the *mise-en-scène*.   Thus the protagonist was
a person of great importance, nor did he always abstain
from making his fellow-artists feel his superiority.

The   deuteragonist,   as   we   have   said,   acted   the
secondary parts, but these were frequently very important.   Thus, if in *Antigone* the title rôle, a
proud   warm-hearted   young   maiden,   in   whom   the
principal interest centres, is decidedly a protagonist's
part, the masterful and hard-hearted Creon is hardly
less important, and constitutes a much larger part.   We
find in many of the tragedies—and still more in the
comedies—several figures which, without commanding
the chief interest, are yet very important to the action,
and very difficult to represent.   In fact, the task of the
deuteragonist required both technically skilled and
talented men, and could not be adequately performed by
mere "utility-men."

As to the tritagonists, however, it does not seem as
if they can be considered as having been much more.
They performed dignified kings, passionless heralds, and
similar parts, which did not require any strong emotional
acting ;   only a good voice, good looks, and faultless
elocution.   Other subordinate parts which necessitated
lively acting, and which had to command the interest as

long as those who performed them remained on the stage, were not confided to the tritagonist, but had frequently to be performed by a protagonist, who was obliged to change mask and costume, and after having undergone the hero's or the heroine's sad fate, to appear in a messenger's dress, and report the circumstances of the death of the same heroic person.   Thus the part of the tritagonist was not very interesting, and its performer not particularly admired.   Aeschines, the orator, was originally an actor of the tritagonist class, and was constantly taunted by his famous antagonist, Demosthenes, with his unsuccessful theatrical career.   We must say it was more on account of his having been a *bad* tritagonist that Demosthenes scourged him than on account of his having merely performed these parts.   If we are to credit Demosthenes, he was so bad that once when he played in *Thyestes*, the audience first hissed, then drove him off the stage, and finally was on the point of stoning him—all from disgust at his acting.   We understand that Aeschines, instead of exposing himself a second time to being thus literally killed by criticism, chose another career, and turned his back on the ungrateful art.

Otherwise, actors, as a class, enjoyed high consideration in Greece.   As has been sufficiently pointed out, a dramatic performance was a religious act ; therefore those who took part in it were considered as the servants of religion, as a kind of priests (fig. 38).

In the early days of the drama the performances were still too rare to allow of forming a real professional class of actors.   The poets acted personally in their own plays, and the few assistants they engaged for single performances in the course of the year were not yet sufficient to constitute a class; they might rather be called amateurs, though they probably spent both time and efforts on their training.   But later the performances became more frequent and extended all over the country, while hitherto they had mostly been confined to Athens.   Even in the adjoining countries and in foreign provinces it became the custom to play Greek dramas. Alexander the Great carried Greek acting companies with him to India, as even on his war expeditions he did not wish to dispense with the enjoyment of this noble art, which he appreciated so highly at home.   The consequence was that the demand for actors constantly increased, and that soon a class of professional scenic or *Dionysiac*[1] artists was trained.   The latter term was used by themselves in honour of the god in whose service they acted.

Even as early as the fourth century B.C. the members of the theatrical profession formed guilds for the protection of their personal rights and interests. These guilds included not only actors, but also dramatic authors, *choreutai*, teachers of the chorus, musicians, even persons of whom costumes were hired.   Through their union these corporations gradually obtained considerable privileges and special favours for their members.   Thus actors had the right at any time to go to foreign, even to hostile states to play comedies, and even in times of war their persons and property were sacred and inviolable.   Later, the guilds also suc-

---

[1] οἱ περὶ τὸν Διόνυσον (or Διονυσιακοὶ) τεχνῖται.

ceeded in obtaining immunity from military service for
their members, a favour which had long been refused,
but which they thought was their due on account of
the religious character of their profession.   A decree
granting these privileges was passed by the council of
the Greek federation, and a copy of it, engraved on
stone, was erected in the Theatre of Dionysus at Athens.
Some of the items of this remarkable decree, which is
fortunately preserved, ran as follows : " It has been
resolved by the Amphictyonic Council that security of
person and property, and exemption from arrest during
peace and war, be ensured to the artists of Dionysus
at Athens ; . . . that they enjoy that exemption from
military service, and that personal security which have
previously been granted to them by the whole Greek
nation ; that the artists of Dionysus be exempt from
military service, in order that they may hold the
appointed celebrations in honour of the gods at the
proper seasons, and be released from other business,
and consecrated to the service of the gods ; that it be
unlawful to arrest or seize an artist of Dionysus in time
of war or peace, unless for debt due to a city or a
private person ; that if an artist be arrested in violation
of these conditions, the person who arrests him, and
the city in which the violation of the law occurs, be
brought to account before the Amphictyonic Council ;
that the immunity from service and personal security
which are granted by the Amphictyonic Council to the
artists of Dionysus at Athens be perpetual ; that the
secretaries cause a copy of this decree to be engraved
on a stone pillar and erected in the temple, and another

sealed copy of the same to be sent to Athens, in order
to show the Athenians that the Amphictyonic Council
are deeply concerned in the observance of religious
duties at Athens, and are ready to accede to the
requests of the artists of Dionysus, and to ratify their
present privileges, and confer such other benefits upon
them as may be possible." [1]

As we see, this decree was granted to the actors'
guild at Athens ; but soon after guilds established on
the same principles were formed throughout the country,
all of which greatly helped to increase the consideration
of the class and to improve its conditions.   Otherwise
we find no information, or scarcely any, about their
pecuniary conditions, terms of engagement, etc.   Prominent protagonists were frequently able to gain wealth
by their art.   Their salaries seem to have been considerable.   Thus Polus is reported to have received
one talent, about £240, for only two days' performances,
terms which would be thought acceptable even by
exacting modern stars.   The inferior actors and the
choreutai of course were not particularly well paid,
and often led a vagabond life with irregular habits,
which lowered their reputation.   The protagonist might
also appear as a kind of theatrical lessee to the
state, undertaking the obligation to provide actors
for all the parts in the play and to pay them.   As
contractor he alone was remunerated by the state, and
very likely—after the fashion of contractors—he did not
pocket the smallest share for himself.   The small companies who roamed about the country and played for

[1] Haigh's translation, *Attic theatre*, p. 253.

whatever payment they could get, of course, here as elsewhere, had the worst time of it.   To these companies especially the guilds had to stretch out their protecting hand, and provide the homeless with a roof when they returned from their tours.   For this purpose, indeed, there was a house, and the guild also provided particular rooms for rehearsing.   The guilds were headed by a chairman, *hiereus* (originally "priest"), who was assisted by a kind of paymaster, *epimelêtês*, and other functionaries.[1]

The technical education of the actors to some extent depended on the particular articles of costume which it was traditional for the performers to wear.   To these special parts belonged above all the *mask*, which constituted a fundamental difference of character between Greek and modern dramatic art.   The mask is one of the attributes of ancient representative art.   Legend credits Thespis with its invention, but its use is probably of far more ancient date, belonging to a time when it was the custom to disguise the assistants at religious festivals with a cover of leaves, to smear their skin with dregs or body-colour, thus making them look quite fantastic, like messengers from a strange superhuman world.   Therefore the use of the mask was originally confined to the merely religious celebrations, the tragedies, whereas the jolly fellows of the comedy appeared with bare faces.   But the stage-masks, as we find them in historical times, were generally made of linen, covered with plaster or a similar material, though they might also be of wood or bark.   They differ from modern masks in covering not only the face but the

[1] Oehmichen : *Bühnenw*, p. 206.

whole head.[1]   They were put on like a helmet with a visor, and tied with a ribbon under the chin.   A large opening was cut out for the mouth, and two smaller ones for the eyes.   The whole mask was superhuman in size, so that the apertures through which the eyes were to look out were sometimes produced only by boring holes through the pupils of the mask, while the iris and other parts of the eyes were painted (fig. 39).

For the rest, the masks were modelled and painted with great care, according to the character they had to represent, and there were special mask-makers (fig. 44), who, of course, were of great importance to the theatre, as they had to depict the whole character of the figure, so to say, by one mimic expression.   Beard and hair were made of real hair, wool or similar material.   On some of the tragic masks we see a projection beneath the hair; it is called *onkos*, and its purpose is to heighten the stature of the figure at the top, as the *cothurnus* added to its size at the bottom.

In forming the masks their makers knew well how to impart to each figure the general stamp which corresponded with each kind of drama.   Nobody would mistake a comic for a tragic mask; the satyric play had its particular snub-nosed and bushy heads.   Passions and peculiarities were characterised in a primitive manner by broad distinct features; profound despair, with updrawn eyebrows, drooping mouth, long vertical furrows on the cheeks, and deep wrinkles in the forehead gives a general image of suffering (figs. 40 and 43);

[1] Face-masks, indeed, were also known, but it is doubtful whether they were used in the theatre.

38

39

38—A celebrated actor whose name is being immortalised.
39—The mask is tried on.

and the broad grimacing mouth of the comedy with a multitude of laughing lines, in fact the whole character-isation, at once places us in the wanton licentious fancy world of Aristophanes (figs. 41 and 42).

On the whole it was necessary to generalise the figures by their masks. Gradually tragedy adopted certain typical masks which were constantly in use, though, of course, each prominent actor or poet con-tributed his share to the appearance of new forms.

Pollux, the authority frequently used in the study of Greek theatrical matters, supplies us with a detailed description of the different typical masks and their signification. But we regret that this description does not agree with the illustrations known. He mentions twenty-eight character-masks for the tragedy: six old men, eight young men, eleven women, and three ser-vants. The Old Comedy did not possess proper typical masks; it used either portrait-masks or caricatures. Fantastic animal masks were also frequently employed in the Old Comedy. For *The Birds* more than fifty different masks were made; they had human features, but large beaks and tufts of feathers (comp. fig. 34). When *The Knights*, the first play which Aristophanes produced under his own name, was to be performed, the poet wished that the mask of the Paphlagonian should be a portrait of the ruler, Cleon, but no mask-maker dared comply with this request; so he had to be con-tented with the features of an ordinary slave. Other-wise, portrait masks were frequent in the representation of Aristophanes. Euripides appears in several of the comedies, and is always represented as an affected and ludicrous person; most likely the mask corresponded with the author's conception of the man, presenting a ludicrous caricature of the gloomy features of the great tragedian. In *The Clouds* Socrates was portrayed, and it is reported that the wise philosopher, instead of taking offence at the caricature, during the performance, while his counterfeit moved on the stage, rose deliberately from his seat and remained standing in order to allow the spectators to judge of the likeness.

Among the twenty-eight typical masks of the tragedy, which belonged to every well-provided theatrical wardrobe, we may mention the "*white man*," an old man's head with flying white hair and full beard; another mask of an old man had a tightly-cropped beard and white smoothly combed hair (fig. 42). The "*black man*" was a mask with dark complexion, black curly hair and beard, and a high *onkos* (tuft of hair); the black man was mostly used for parts of tyrants, *e.g.*, Creon, or, in general, for the strong mature man, Hercules, Oedipus, etc. The youthful mask had light hair, raised eyebrows, and fair complexion. Of female masks there was the *old woman* with long flowing hair, the *young maiden* with very fair complexion and short curly hair parted in the middle, the *newly married wife* with rosy complexion and long wavy hair, etc., etc.

Besides these general types which might serve in all pieces, there were also a number of a more special character, which could only be used by some particular figure. Thus the mask of the *blind soothsayer*, which was employed for Teiresias, the mask of the *many-eyed Argus*, painted with a multitude of eyes, the mask of

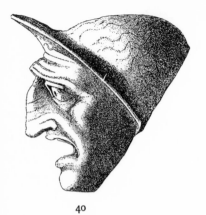

40

40

41

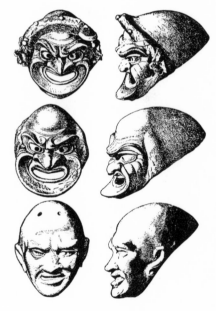

42

40—Tragic masks.　　　　　　　　**41**—Comic mask.

　　42—Types of old men and masks of parasites.

Actæon with the horns, and so forth. The total number of such special masks is stated to have been thirty. Sometimes also it may have been necessary to change masks during the play, as when Helena in the play of Euripides returns to the stage with close-cut hair,[1] or when Oedipus appears with blood-stained, blinded face.

Though the figures of the New Comedy were every-day types, taken from the most trivial spheres of real life, and had not an atom of fantastic or mythical origin attached to them, the use of the mask was so insepar-ably combined with the Greek stage, that it could not even be dispensed with in these unfantastic pictures of real life. Nay, it retained its queer twisted and highly exaggerated appearance, which might be very appropriate for the burlesque of ancient comedy, but was somewhat out of keeping with the realistic figures of the new pictures of society which, as it seems, would have gained by the adoption of a less conventional costume, and especially by the expressive play of the living face. Perhaps it was thought that such play would have been lost in the immense space of the theatres ; perhaps con-vention, which was always very strong in theatrical matters, did not allow of a breach of the old custom : so much is certain, that no piece was ever performed without masks.

The masks of the New Comedy were still more conventional than those of tragedy, and seldom went

[1] Thou, why hast thou attired thee in dark robes,
    Thy white cast off, and from thy queenly head
    Hast thou with sweep of steel thy tresses shorn
    And wetted with fast-streaming tears thy cheeks
    Weeping ?

(Arthur S. Way.)

beyond the fixed types which recurred in all pieces. Pollux gives a list of forty-four comic masks, nine of which were for old men, eleven for young men, seven for slaves, three for old women, and fourteen for young girls. Each of these divisions contained different varieties, which, by the colour of hair and beard, the shape of mouth and eyebrows, etc., indicated the character which was to be represented.

The roguish slave — the Scapin type — invariably had the same red hair and impudent features; the harsh old father had the same bald head and furious expression; the warriors always wore large bushy wigs, while thick curly hair indicated the mature man, and close-cropped hair the slave or old man. Thus also the pale complexion was typical of the lover or the sick man; the rogues had red cheeks as well as red hair; warriors and country people were of a sunburnt brown colour. A common feature of all the decidedly comic masks was the large funnel-shaped aperture for the mouth, which most of all helped to give the physiognomy its stamp of grotesque caricature, whereas the masks of male and female lovers, with their fine regular features, came closer to the tragic type.

The *costume* used in tragedies was quite conventional, and differed entirely from everyday dress. The tragic subjects, with very few exceptions, were derived from myth and hero lore, so their principal characters were nearly always of *superhuman* nature. Therefore in the costume no imitation of reality was attempted; on the contrary, its object was to produce an impression of something unusual, unreal, and thereby

43

43

44

43—Tragic masks.   **44**—Mask-maker.

sublime. The tragic costume, such as it remained essentially unaltered till the latest times, is said to have been introduced in this shape by Aeschylus, who, it is supposed, imitated the dress—no doubt of Oriental origin—which was worn by the priests of the Eleusinian mysteries.

The costume appointed by Aeschylus consisted of a long many-coloured and elaborately designed garment, the *chitôn*, which was the same for men and women, and over it was worn a long gaudy mantle or cloak (figs. 45 and 46). The real tragic *chitôn* was called *poikilon*; it reached down to the feet, and was either woven in horizontal (sometimes vertical) stripes, or elaborately embroidered with ornaments and figures. In contrast to everyday dress, the tragic garment had long sleeves which came down to the hands. High up under the breast a belt, frequently ornamented with gold and brilliant stones, gathered in the garment, thus forming it into long folds by which the figure increased in size (fig. 48). Characters belonging to the lower classes wore a shorter *chitôn*; soothsayers—*e.g.*, Teiresias—were clothed in a net-like woollen garment, and warriors as well as hunters had one arm wrapped up in a cloth or shawl of a blood-red shade. In colour the dresses were generally light and bright, so as to produce an impression of splendour and gorgeousness. In some tragedies, however, it became the fashion to go to the opposite extreme. Thus Aristophanes taunts his tragic colleague Euripides with the paltry rags which he allows his piteous heroes to drag about on the stage.[1] Fugitives wore dirty or

[1] Aristophanes: *Acharnians*, v. 410-480.

grey, sometimes also green or blue, garments. Kings
generally appeared holding their sceptres (fig. 47); old
people leant on staves with bent handles.

Head-coverings, as a rule, were not worn on the stage,
any more than in real life; on the top of the tragic mask
with its *onkos* it would indeed have been difficult to
wear an additional headgear. As an exception, however,
travellers were represented with hats; Hermes also
appeared with his broad-brimmed *petasos*, and sailors and
old men occasionally wore head-coverings. Performers
of female rôles on certain occasions pulled their over-
garments over their head, and also used veils and hair-
bands (*mitra*). Garlands were worn among others by
those who brought joyful messages from the Delphic
Oracle, or those who were invited to banquets.

A peculiar characteristic of the tragedy was the well-
known *cothurnus*, which even to this day is the typical
expression for the high tragic style ("to wear the
cothurnus"). By-the-bye, *cothurnus* is the Roman, not
the Greek term for this famous boot; its Greek name is
embatês. The *cothurnus* was a high boot with an immensely thick wooden sole, intended to add to the stature
of the actor, thus enabling him to surpass the members
of the chorus in height. Therefore the thickness of
the sole was in proportion to the rank of the person.
The soles were square blocks, of equal size for both
feet (figs. 45, 46 and 47). We do not suppose, however,
that by this means the tragedian added more than five
or six inches to his height. In order to establish the
right proportion between the bulk and the artificial height
of the figure, padding was used on breast and stomach,

45—Tragic actor in full costume.

and sometimes the hands were magnified by a peculiar kind of large gloves.

That these strangely equipped large figures with their immovable faces, which seemed petrified with suffering, and in their gorgeous splendour, advancing slowly with solemn measured movements, must have produced a powerful and romantic impression on the minds of the naïve ancient Greeks, we can easily imagine. They must have appeared almost like living images of the gods, and when the people heard the beautiful grave words emanating from these walking statues, they were seized with artistic as well as religious enthusiasm. But the times could not continue equally pious and naïve, nor did the tragedies for ever remain of the same sublime nature, seeking their subjects far beyond the realities of the day. Times came when the old means of producing effect ought to have been dis-carded, so as to make room for others which would have harmonised better with the new taste and the new poetry. Instead of this, the old tragic equipment was adhered to with the strictest loyalty and respect down to the last days of classical antiquity; and the conse-quence was that that which had been sublime now seemed ludicrous, what had been overwhelming became disturbing. Lucian only expresses the thoughts of his time when he ridicules the enormous stilts on which the tragic actors march, and wonders how they can get safely across the stage. He makes fun of their paddings on chest and stomach, and of their "hollow mouths which look as if they were going to swallow the audience." We see from a story in Philostratus that as late as the third century, a quite naïve public could still be strongly impressed—though not in the way intended—by the apparition of these strange figures.

A Greek company of actors came to a country in Spain where plays had never been seen before. The honest country people were struck dumb with amazement and secret horror on seeing the tragedian advance on the stage with his mighty body and his immovable face, with the enormous open mouth. But when he lifted up his voice and began to speak with the sonorous clang of the tragic declamation, there was a general panic among the public; all rushed out of the theatre horror-stricken, as if he had been a demon.

As to the costume in the satyric play—the dress of the chorus has been already described — that of the principal characters was the same as in the tragedy; only the *chitôn* was shorter, to prevent it from impeding animated wanton action. The *cothurnus* was dispensed with, probably for the same reason, though we cannot draw this inference from the illustrations, as, from artistic considerations, it is frequently omitted even in pictures of tragedians. Old Silenus, a constantly recurring figure in the satyr play, wears a sort of tights trimmed with a regular design of hairy or woollen tufts scattered all over the body, except hands, feet and head; sometimes also he is depicted with a garment and trousers of hairy skin. Hides of panthers, harts and goats were frequently used in the satyric play, but the panther skins were imitations, as the real ones were too expensive to buy.

About the costumes in the Old Comedy we do not

46

47

5—Female costume in tragedy (from a mosaic).   47—King in tragedy (from a mosaic).

know much, at any rate nothing very trustworthy. There are no illustrations extant of the Aristophanic period, but there are a series of vase-paintings from Lower Italy representing scenes out of the Graeco-Italian burlesque comedies of the *Phlyakes*, which, having sprung from the old Doric mask plays, exhibited great resemblance to the plays of Aristophanes; the phallic element especially was common to both kinds. Some of the paintings would even seem to be direct representations of Aristophanic scenes thus—fig. 50, the opening scene of the Frogs. In so far, then, as these actors of Greek origin really represented the old Greek comedy, it is natural to think that they also preserved the traditional costume, considering the tendency to adhere to old forms, of which Greek theatrical institutions bear witness everywhere. The Phlyakian vase-paintings for the most part date from the third century B.C. In these representations of dramatic scenes we are particularly struck by the strange character of the male costume, which seems to be derived from the worship of Dionysus. Most remarkable are the long tight-fitting trousers worn by all the male characters, which in some of the figures are supplemented by jackets with long sleeves of the same design and colours (figs. 49-53). These garments are not Greek at all, and, like the tragic costume, probably came from Asia. So they are purely conventional loans from divine worship, and not imitations of the dresses of everyday life. Over this tight-fitting dress, which as a rule was transversely striped, but of different colours, they wore a jerkin without sleeves, somewhat like the fencing habit which is used nowadays, with exaggerated paddings on stomach and hind part. This jerkin was frequently flesh-coloured, being thus designed in order to represent the naked body (comp. fig. 50), and a phallus—inseparable from the Old Comedy—of red leather and grotesque form was fastened to it. The female costumes were more like the ordinary dress (comp. fig. 54). Instead of the *cothurnus*, the foot was covered with a shoe which came up to the ankle.

The scenic attire of the New Comedy was essentially like the ordinary Greek dress, as was indeed appropriate to the everyday types of these dramas. Yet even in this matter the Greek tendency to generalisation showed itself. By all sorts of outward marks the costume of the New Comedy classified its persons. These marks generally had a remote connection with reality, but their principal object was to guide the audience, which gradually learned that such and such external attributes belonged to such and such a character. The material or cut of the clothes marked the distinction between a citizen and a rustic (the latter wore a leather tunic and carried a wallet and staff), between the youth and the old man, the respectable woman and the courtesan, who appeared in a brilliant variegated costume, with em-broidered mantle and golden ribbon in her hair (figs. 55 and 56).

There were particular costumes for the happy and for the ill-fated man, for the exile, and for the young girl who had sinned against the laws of chastity. This regularity was carried beyond all limits of probability, each character having its complete uniform, which became part of the figure and inseparable from it. The

48

49

48—Medea, her children and the pedagogue (scene from a tragedy).
49—Scene from a comedy (vase painting).

warrior always wore his purple mantle, the cook never removed his coarse kitchen apron, the parasite always wore a dark mantle fastened up, ready to run after a good dinner; the procuress in her gaudy outlandish dress invariably betrayed her foreign extraction. Even the burglar and the courtesan's maid at first sight revealed their position in society and in the play.

In Greek dramatic art we notice three modes of delivery: (1) *ordinary recitation*—speech without accompaniment of music, but supported by gestures; (2) *song* —accompanied by flute or harp, and supported by dancing; (3) the *melodramatic recitation* called *parakatalogê*, which consisted in a rhythmic declamation supported by flute and gesticulation, occasionally also by dancing.

In all species of drama the *iambic trimeter* was spoken; the purely lyrical passages were sung, and all the remainder was uttered in *parakatalogê*.[1]

Of the manner in which songs and melodramatic recitation were delivered no accounts are extant. All we know is—as stated above in mentioning choral performances —that polyphonous song was unknown. As to speech and ordinary recitation, a very particular training was required, and each performance had to be studied with the minutest care. A very flexible, strongly accented and intelligible diction were indispensable qualifications of the performer, more especially as he had to do without the help of varying facial expression, which in our dramatic art is such a valuable help to declamation; indeed, a glance or a smile often conveys more expression than the finest voice.

[1] Comp. Oehmichen: p. 272 ff.; Alb. Müller, p. 189 ff.; Haigh, p. 241 ff.

As to mere speech it was urgent that the Greek—at least the Athenian—actor should use the finest Athenian pronunciation without any alloy of dialect or foreign accent. He had also to be very particular about rhythm. If he was unfortunate enough to add or to forget a syllable, or to break the rhythm and spoil the verse by a mistaken accent, the audience would protest with a storm of disapproval. The first and foremost requirement, however, was a naturally strong and perfectly trained *voice*. Though the immense theatres are proved to have possessed wonderfully good acoustic facilities, it was no trifling affair to speak to an audience of about thirty thousand people; and though the funnel-shaped mouth of the mask perhaps added to the power of the voice, it also weakened the articulation and, together with the conditions of space, generally necessitated slow speech. Of course the speed had to be adapted to the character of the play, to the situation or the part. In tragedy it was always slower, in comedy quicker. But besides the requirements as to elocution and metre, display of power and observation of time, great value was attributed to the care with which delicate shades of enunciation, changes of pitch, pauses and accents, were adapted to the words.

As the Greek actor was at the same time singer, dancer and reciter, he required a very thorough technical education, especially since the costume presented obstacles to all his acquirements. The mask impeded his speech and his song, the paddings and the long folds of his garments hindered his gesticulation, and the *cothurnus* necessitated great calculation in walking and dancing.

50

51

50—Scene from the *Frogs*, by Aristophanes.
51—Scene from a comedy (vase painting).

The public was very exacting with regard to correctness and skill; its critical faculty was awake to the slightest fault, and merciless to the most trifling mishap. For years Aeschines had to hear himself reviled because, while he was an actor, he had once happened to fall and to be helped up by the teacher of the chorus.[1] Even though long practice might enable the actor to move pretty freely on his high *cothurni*, they were bound to occasion a slow, not very lively, gait, which, we must say, was quite appropriate to the tragedy. Then again the movements of the hands were developed to a perfection and with a well-calculated variety of minutiae, which are scarcely equalled in our modern gesticulation, and which almost compensated for the lack of facial play. Unfortunately we possess no thorough expositions of this branch of technique, which no doubt might give most interesting details and hints instructive even to our own time.

But, first and last, it was the training of the *voice* which received attention. A good voice in Greece was almost synonymous with a good actor. In this respect also the Greek actor may be compared with our operatic singers. He is judged more by his voice than by his histrionic talent. Demosthenes said that actors should be judged by their voices, politicians by their wisdom. It was—at any rate with the general public—the power even more than the beauty of the voice that was decisive. Extraordinary phenomena have at all times exercised

[1] This was the part of Oinomaos in the tragedy of the same name, during a performance in one of the provinces. Therefore Demosthenes called his antagonist the "boorish Oinomaos."

an overwhelming influence on the naïve public; and
as nowadays the deep C of the bass or the F *in alt.*
of the soprano never fail of their effect, so two thousand
years ago exulting cheers hailed the actor who could
shake the drums of sixty thousand ears with the tremendous roars of his voice.   So besides plastic exercises,
the scenic education consisted essentially in the training
of the voice, but this training was indeed carried on with
the utmost perseverance.

The actors generally practised their voice early in
the morning before eating, because immediately after
a meal it is less flexible.[1] Temperance in eating and
drinking was considered necessary for him who desired
to have full control over his voice; some authorities also
advised abstinence from love relations. Throughout the
whole of antiquity the Greek actors were celebrated for
the perseverance with which they cultivated the technique of the throat. Cicero reports how they would
spend years in practising declamation in a sitting
posture, and how before and after the performance they
schooled their voices in different attitudes in order to
harden it against all fatigues. The mode of their representation, which was frequently accompanied by dancing,
or at least by posing in various attitudes, rendered it
necessary that song and speech should not be impeded
by the difficulties which elaborately twisted limbs and
wild gambols—such as were used in comedy—present
to those who are only accustomed to sing and to speak
in a still, upright posture.

---

[1] Modern teachers also recommend this hour for practising, especially
for passage-singing.

52

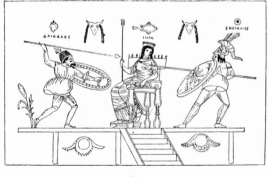

53

52, 53--Scenes from comedies.

We also find professional teachers of voice-training. Such a teacher was called *phonaskos*, and as a support in the purely musical portions of the performance, such a technical expert was also present at the representations to act as a director; with a special instrument (*phonas-kikon-organon*) he indicated the tone and beat time.

Besides individual education and practice, of course there were also common practices and collective rehearsals. These rehearsals, however, strange to say, did not take place in the theatre—perhaps because in the open space outsiders would have been able to overhear them—but in houses specially appropriated to the purpose; and it is equally remarkable that the players did not appear in costume or mask [1] at any of the rehearsals, not even at the last "dress"-rehearsal, *proagon*, which was held a few days before the festival itself.

Information about particular actors and characteristics of their art are only found in scattered remarks in ancient authors; and the picture that can be drawn from these sketchy and desultory observations is very incomplete. So much, however, we think, may be inferred, that Greek dramatic art may be divided into *three periods*. The first of these periods is connected with Aeschylus as the chief actor and manager of his own plays, and his two assistants Kleander (deuteragonist) and Mynniscus (tritagonist). We must imagine the art of this period as strictly conventional, formal and dignified, superior to naturalistic effects, with a solemn and monotonous, yet warm and expressive declamation and symbolic dancing motions—we might say more like a

[1] Comp. Oehmichen, *op. cit.* 264 f.

recital than a dramatic performance. About the histrionic talent of Aeschylus himself we know nothing, but we may take for granted that it bore the stamp of his superiority. He was born in Eleusis,[1] the Eleusis of the Mysteries, the hearth of Greek religious cult, and he was descended from an old distinguished family. Naturally endowed with deep and grand poetic gifts, he was just the man to impart to dramatic art the solemn religious stamp which it bore throughout this period; nor was it till after his death that new currents made their appearance. At the time when political orators, who had hitherto observed a similar calm and monotonous dignity, became more lively, and, instead of contenting themselves, like Pericles, with standing stiffly in their carefully draped garments, thrust aside their mantle and accompanied their words with animated gestures—a custom which Cleon had invented —at that time, we say, new blood streamed into the veins of dramatic art. New forms were required, approaches were made to the modes of expression used in real life; stiffness and uniformity were discarded. These innovations, of course, scandalised the performers who adhered to the school of Aeschylus—such is the course of the world; a proof hereof is left us in an observation of Mynniscus, who survived Aeschylus many years, thus having the grief of seeing the traditional principles violated by the new school. He accused Kallipides, one of the most eager adherents of the modern school, of being an "ape," because he copied nature instead of conforming himself to tradition.

[1] About the year 525 B.C.

54

55

55

56

54—Scene from a comedy.
55—Types from the later comedy : slave, courtesan and procuress.
56—Scene of a later comedy.

The same Kallipides *was* indeed something of a monkey. We find several examples of his foolish vanity, when at the return of Alcibiades to his native country in 408 B.C., the actor stood on his ship in full scenic attire, and with a mighty voice shouted out his orders to the rowers ; or when at a meeting with the Spartan king Agesilaus, in his surprise at not being received with due enthusiasm, he placed himself before the king and exclaimed : "Don't you know me, oh king?" Upon which Agesilaus replied with genuine laconicism : "Yes, are you not the coxcomb Kallipides?" Later he made an offer to the king to show his skill by imitating the song of the nightingale, but the king stopped him with the words : "I have heard the bird itself." Apart from these follies Kallipides was considered a really distinguished tragedian, who, together with Nicostratus, paved the way to the new time. Nicostratus was particularly noted for the art with which he delivered the long messages so frequent in the Greek tragedy. His acting was so perfect that it became proverbial to say as special praise : "He does it like Nicostratus!" Sophocles himself never gained distinction as an actor ; his weak voice compelled him to leave the stage early, and after his time it ceased to be the fashion for poets to act in their own plays.

But it was after the time of Sophocles that dramatic art began to flourish independently. About the actors of Sophocles himself, Kleidemides and Tlepolemus, we know nothing but the names. But contemporarily with Demosthenes a number of names appear, *e.g.*, Polus, Theodorus, Aristodemus, Neoptolemus, Thessalus, Athenodorus, and others, which mark the *Second Period*, that of the great virtuosi, in contrast with the first—the period of subordination, general effect, declamation.

Of Polus, whom Plutarch places above all contemporary performers in nobility, heroic dignity and expression of feeling, an anecdote is related which characterises the whole class. Polus had lost a son whom he deeply loved   Shortly after this bereavement he acted Electra in Sophocles' tragedy of this name. In this play, as we know, a scene occurs in which Electra, holding in her hand the urn in which she supposes the ashes of Orestes to be contained, has to give vent in a long speech to her grief at his death.[1]

[1] (Soph. *Electra*, v. 1099-1143):—

O monument of him whom o'er all else
I loved ! sole relic of Orestes' life,
How cold in this thy welcome is the hope
Wherein I decked thee as I sent thee forth !
Then I beheld thee radiant, whom I now
Bear lightly, a mere nothing, in my hands.
Would I had passed from life ere I despatched
Thee from my arms, that saved thee, to a land
Of strangers, stealing thee from death !   For then
Thou hadst been quiet on that far-off day,
And had thy portion in our father's tomb.
Now thou hast perished miserably, afar
From home and from thy sister, in exile.
And I, O wretchedness ! neither have bathed
And laid thee forth, nor from the blazing fire
Collected the sad burden as was meet :
But thou, when foreign hands have tended thee,
Cam'st, a small handful, in a narrow shell.
Woe for the constant care I spent on thee
Of old all vainly, with sweet toil !   For never
Wast thou thy mother's darling, nay, but mine,
And I of all the household most thy nurse,
While sister, sister, was thy voice to me.
But now all this is vanished in one day.
Aging in thy death.   Thou hast carried all away
As with a whirlwind, and art gone.   No more

In order to put himself into the right state of feeling, Polus, instead of using the ordinary object employed in the theatre, took the urn containing the ashes of his own son, and holding it in his hand, declaimed his monologue with so genuine and deep emotion that the audience was extraordinarily impressed. There is something repulsive in this merely outward means of soliciting applause, the effect of which on the spectators can only have been due to the circumstance that they knew the real state of things. Still the very fact that the actor did not recoil from using—though in a mistaken and inartistic way—his most sacred personal griefs in the service of his art, shows that the task of the dramatic performer was considered as a very serious matter at this period. Polus, we may add, was teacher of rhetoric to Demosthenes.

> My father lives : thyself art lost in death :
> I too am dead in thee. Our enemies
> Triumph, and she is maddened with her joy,
> Our mother most unmotherly, of whom
> Thy secret missives often told me thou
> Wouldst rise to be the punisher.
> The hapless genius of thy lot and mine
> Hath reft away, and given thee thus to me,—
> For thy loved form thy dust and fruitless shade.
> O bitterness ! O piteous sight ! Woe ! woe !
> Oh ! sent on thy dire journey, dearest one,
> How thou hast ruined me ! Thou hast indeed,
> Dear brother ! Then receive me to thyself,
> Hide me in this thy covering there to dwell,
> Me who am nothing, with thy nothingness,
> For ever ! Yea, when thou wert here above,
> I ever shared with thee in all, and now
> I would not have thee shut me from thy tomb.
> O let me die and follow thee ! the dead,
> My mind assures me now, have no more pain.

(Lewis Campbell.)

Theodorus was particularly admired on account of his rare gift of expressing feelings in the most natural way, and the most critical experts therefore considered him as the first in his own line of art. Aristotle says of him that while all the other actors seem to speak with somebody else's voice, he alone speaks with his own, and for this reason produces the greatest effect. Once at a performance in Thessaly the hard and brutal tyrant, Alexander of Thera, was moved to tears by the naturalness of his acting, and had to leave the theatre in order to conceal his emotion. He afterwards told Theodorus that he had felt ashamed to be seen weeping at the simulated grief of an actor, while the real sufferings of his own people left him insensible. The most noted parts of Theodorus were Orestes and Antigone.

The fame of Aristodemus and Neoptolemus is especially connected with Philip of Macedonia, at whose court they were highly esteemed as artists and as men. The Macedonian king even entrusted them with diplomatic missions, and they had a considerable share in the conclusion of the Peace of Philocrates. This transaction, however, exposed them to severe accusations of treason by Demosthenes, who thought they had acted more in the interest of Philip than in that of their countrymen. It is said of Aristodemus as well as of Polus that he copied well-known statues in his poses.

The favourite actor of Alexander the Great was Thessalus. On Alexander's return from Egypt a great tragic contest was held at Tyre, where the kings of Cyprus acted as *chorêgi*, and the leaders of the army as judges. At this competition appeared among others the

two tragedians Athenodorus and Thessalus. To the
great annoyance of Alexander, Athenodorus won the
prize. The monarch declared that he would willingly
have given a part of his kingdom to secure Thessalus
the victory.

All the actors here mentioned were tragedians.
About the comic actors we know very little except a
few names, such as Hermon, Apollodorus (protagonist in
The Peace of Aristophanes), Philemon, Satyrus (who is
said to have acted slaves), Parmenon, Nausicrates and
Lycon. Comic talent was scarcely so highly appreciated
as tragic, nor do we suppose the humour to have been
of the most delicate sort. For instance, one of Hermon's
best jokes was to knock the heads of his fellow-actors
with his stick, and Parmenon won his laurels by his
exceptional skill in imitating the grunting of a hog. The
tragedian Theodorus assured the comic actor Satyrus that
it was much easier to make the people laugh than to
make them weep, and we may suppose that comic art to
a great extent consisted in childish buffoonery.

After the time of Alexander a *Third Period* began
for the Greek drama, a distinct period of decline. The
delicate Attic taste was spoiled by barbarous invasions,
and the requirements of the public assumed a tendency towards grotesque display of power and empty
naturalism. The actors, who, even during the preceding
period, had evinced a disposition for virtuoso-like artificial
tricks of voice, did not disdain to excel in mere spiritless
imitations of natural sounds. They won fame by copying the roaring of the sea, the rolling of a carriage,
the splashing of rain, and similar frivolities ; imitations of

animals became favourite ingredients of the plays, and at the same time an exaggerated gesticulation helped to destroy the noble simplicity of style which had been the essential characteristic of Greek dramatic art.

V

THE "SUPERS"

Mute and Subordinate Actors.

IN tragedy as well as comedy there was need of subordinate actors to undertake the parts which could not be performed by the three *hypokritai*, as well as those of ordinary mutes.   Kings, queens and other distinguished persons were constantly attended by a considerable suite of magnificently dressed "supers" who, though not requiring a difficult technical training like that of the prominent actors, had to possess a certain amount of ability in posing, and, inasmuch as they had speeches to recite, some knowledge of the laws of diction.   Occasional mute characters, such as Bia in the *Prometheus* and Hermes in *The Eumenides*, were also represented by *comparsi*.   In so far as the expenses of their training and equipment were defrayed by the *chorêgus*, these artists stood on a level with the *choreutai*, though with respect to their functions they would have to be classed with the actors.   Whether they wore masks like the *hypokritai* and the *choreutai* is not recorded; they probably did.   Flute-players and other musicians were not masked.

VI

COURSE OF THE PERFORMANCE

The Day of the Performance is considered as a General Holiday—Arrival of the Public and its Attitude during the Play—Expression of Approval and of Disapproval.

AT Athens, as in all other Greek cities, the performances began at dawn ; and, as the festival bore the character of a contest between different poets—in later times also between different actors—each of whom produced several pieces, they lasted the whole day. The seats of the spectators were unnumbered, and though the performances were not formally announced beforehand, the crowds that rushed to see them were immense. At Athens there were only a few performances in the course of a year, and they always took place at the Dionysiac festivals ; besides, all minds were so occupied by these events that a special announcement would have been quite superfluous. On these festal days all work was suspended, all shops were closed, and all business was put off ; even imprisoned debtors were set free, and arrests were strictly prohibited. Long before sunrise thousands of expectant people assembled outside the theatre, noisy crowds of men, women and children, all bent upon enjoying themselves, and eager to obtain the best seats. All were in their holiday attire, and wore garlands in honour of the god. Some people also honoured him—and provided for their own refreshment as well—by bringing jugs of wine and baskets of food, if they did not trust to the liberality of the *chorêgus* for providing them.   From religious as well as from practical motives these functionaries frequently distributed copious libations of the fiery Greek wine to impecunious citizens in order to stimulate their enthusiasm for the play, and for the god in whose honour it was performed.   Authors—especially writers of comedies—were also accused of the wily trick of buying the applause of the public by distributing sweets, nuts and fruit.   Aristophanes, who despises such bribery, condemns it in the following lines of *The Wasps* : [1]

"But 'tis time that I say what the theme of our play,
    dropping first through a short admonition."
(*Turns to the spectators.*)

Gentle sirs, for whom we live, at none present here pray
    give to experience and hope too large warrant ;
Nor do courtesy so small as to think his taste shall
    pall on stol'n trash such as Megara sees current.
We've no slave nor serving man, who from basket or
    from pan scatters nuts to the greedy spectators ;
No Hercules who talks of short commons or who
    balks for the joke's sake his keen masticators.
(Mitchell.)

At length the "box-office" is opened, and in rushes the motley crowd ; each person pays his two obols and pushes on with his elbows in order to secure the best seat he can get behind the reserved places.   Fights and bruises were unavoidable, especially at the time when the admission was quite free.   The entrance fee of two

[1] Aristophanes : *The Wasps*, v. 54-59.

obols was introduced on purpose to prevent too great disorder and to keep away the worst elements. Afterwards—under Pericles—it was enacted that the state should supply every citizen who applied for it with the admission fee; of this privilege, however, the wealthier citizens did not avail themselves.

Not till after the less important part of the audience had settled down did the more distinguished citizens go to the theatre, where seats had been secured beforehand by their slaves. Clients and servants carried cushions and rugs to render the hard wood or stone seats more comfortable, or to afford protection against sun or cold. These worthies entered and took possession of their places with grave dignity; the most popular among them were hailed with cheers and clapping of hands; the less favoured had to endure rude taunts and mocking exclamations.

The lowest front rows, which were still empty, were reserved for the archons, the priest of Dionysus and other priests, foreign ambassadors, and such private men as were marked out for especial honour. At last these high dignitaries made their appearance. The priest of Dionysus was conducted to the best seat, a richly ornamented chair in the centre of the front row; the others were grouped round him according to their rank, and at last the theatre was filled. A magnificent sight indeed! The steep mountain slope covered to a giddy height with an assembly of thirty thousand people in festal attire of bright and airy colours, white, yellow, purple, with dark green vine-leaves on their black curls; at the bottom the circle of venerable priests robed in

white ; at the top a whirling and waving crowd of shouting, laughing and gesticulating common people, slaves and
boys ; and above the whole scene the bright deep blue sky
of Greece, towards which the hubbub and clatter of thirty
thousand voices ascend like the humming of a swarm of
bees.   The *orchêstra* alone is still empty and silent.
Suddenly the tones of a flute are heard, the roaring of
the enormous crowd rapidly calms down, and the choral
procession, in fantastic and brilliant array, appears in the
orchêstra, singing and dancing.   The play has begun,
and is listened to in silence and breathless suspense.
The beautiful words of the great poets emanate in
sonorous tones from the strange apparitions on the
stage, and reach up to the outermost tiers of the
immense auditorium ; the simple receptive ears are filled
with beautiful sound, the brains with thoughts, and the
hearts with enthusiasm.   There has been no previous
toil all day long to slacken either enthusiasm or physical
power, such as often reduces our modern theatrical
performances to a kind of after-dinner relaxation ; the
enthusiasm must out, must vent itself in cheers, clapping
of hands, " encores "—demonstrations of applause which,
as we know, have come down to our own time.

But the day is long, and neither poets nor actors are
all equally good.   Moments will come when the audience
feels dull, discontented, scandalised, even furious at a
bad piece or a bad performance, and in these cases
the discontent must out as well as the enthusiasm in the
opposite case.   It cannot be denied that the disapproval
of the Greek public often expressed itself so energetically
that our tame modern way of hissing and the much

hated "cat-call" are nothing in comparison. In Greece hissing was also the usual and mildest form of disapproval, but it was generally accompanied by kicking and loud groaning, a deafening noise which was meant to stop the actor and the play. This done, the next piece was loudly demanded, which often caused disturbance, as the other actors could not well be prepared to act the next play on so short a notice and were not dressed in the proper costume. It was a favourite proceeding to show disapproval of an actor by throwing stones at him, thus condemning his performance and compelling him to retire from the stage. This was the fate of Aeschines, who very nearly lost his life on the occasion. In the country, where minds were less excitable and where fruits were within easy reach, unpopular actors were generally pelted with figs and olives. If the acting was so bad that the public did not find even this punishment severe enough, they roared that the culprit ought to be flogged. And to the general satisfaction — except that of the actor himself — this chastisement was administered by a kind of theatrical police, the "staff-bearers," who, armed with thick staves, assisted at the performances, seated on the *thymèlê*, whence they kept an eye on rioters and pickpockets.

The Greek public was very emotional, soon carried away by enthusiasm and easily scandalised, quick to tears and quick to laughter, susceptible to the sublimest feelings as to the most wanton jokes; but always keeping in view their personal dignity as well as that of the drama, they never tolerated the slightest lack of respect for national events or religious belief. Thus there was a hailstorm of resentment when Euripides opened his tragedy *Melanippe* with these words: "Zeus, whoever Zeus may be, for I do not know it except from rumour," etc.   When Phrynichus, the actor and poet, produced his play *The Conquest of Miletus*, which describes the conquest of this town by the hereditary enemy, the Persians, the audience was so touched that all burst into tears.   The poet, however, was not called forth or crowned, as he possibly expected; on the contrary, he was sentenced to pay one thousand drachmas, because he had ventured to remind the Athenians of one of their national misfortunes, and it was forbidden by law ever to perform the piece again.

The Greek public was as fond of tears as of laughter, of being edified as of being amused.   It did not prefer fun to seriousness.   But one thing was required in both: a festal character.   And as in its outward form the Greek theatrical performance was a festival, so the distinguishing mark of good Greek dramatic art was its deeply impressive solemn and festal stamp

THE ROMAN THEATRE

I

THE DRAMA

Unnational Character of the Roman Drama—Germs of National Dramatic
Production—Introduction of the Greek Drama by Livius Andronicus,
Plautus and Terence—Decline of the Literary Drama—*Atellanae*
and their Types—Immorality of the *Mimes*.

THE Roman drama more than any other, we suppose,
lacked a national stamp. The *Comedy* has a twofold
interest to us in that it not only gives us information about the later Greek comedians, of whom the
Roman ones were only imitators, but also in that it
shows us the material which furnished the subjects used
in the works of our own writers of classical plays. Without Plautus and Terence our knowledge of Menander's
and Philemon's method of working would have been
more than defective, and without these two authors it
is not easy to say what shape the dramatic productions
of Molière and Holberg [1] would have assumed. But if
we had possessed the original Greek comedies, it is
scarcely probable that the Latin Comedy would have
attracted more attention now than the Latin Tragedy,
in which absolutely none but philologists and literary
specialists are interested.

We cannot say, however, that Roman dramatic

[1] A Danish dramatist.

literature is entirely deficient in national colour.   It
originated in rural festivals and religious celebrations,
where, as in Greece and elsewhere, the entertainment
was enlivened by mummeries and merry songs.   Each
province had its masques and its encounters of wit, and
the cleverest and most successful of these works of
course had the widest circulation and superseded the
inferior production.   Thus Fescennium in South Etruria
was famous for its merry harvest festivals in honour of
rustic and silvan divinities, and the wanton Fescennine
wedding songs held their ground as a special branch of
literature down to the time of the Empire.   In Latium
mimetic dances accompanied by comic tales and songs
were eagerly cultivated by the young people.   Out of
these performances arose a kind of primitive drama, the
so-called *satura*, which survived for some time as an
after-play to the later artistic tragedies.   But of still
greater importance were the merry masques which arose
in the small village of Atella in Campania.[1]   The
Atellanae, as they were called, were little improvised
comedies performed by the young villagers under certain
recognised masks, and they were brimful of practical
jokes and witty attacks on local matters.   These mask-
figures gradually developed into fixed comical types
which were so successful that their fame extended to
Rome, and tempted the young Roman citizens to adopt
this new form of entertainment, in which—hidden by the
caricaturing masks—they could permit themselves the
coarsest jokes without exposing their own persons.   The
Atellanae continued to be improvisations in which only

[1] Now Sant' Arpino, a village several miles from Aversa.

the principal features of the action were settled before-hand, while the details of the dialogue were left to the inspiration of the amateur actors. From Magna Graecia came the *Mimes*, also little, originally improvised farces, the only object of which was to excite laughter, but which drew their subjects less from the ridiculous sides of ordinary life than from parodied myths, in which the erotic scenes formed the principal attraction.

All these popular plays contained the germ of a genuine national comedy. But this germ was soon choked, at least it never attained to a healthy or vigorous growth, from the time when the Greek drama took root in Latin soil. When for the first time (in the year B.C. 240) Livius Andronicus produced regular tragedies and comedies, either translations from Greek or compositions after Greek models, the Romans instantly felt, even through the feeble reflection of the great art which Andronicus was capable of giving, that here they stood before a dramatic culture with which their own coarse popular farces could not compete. Though Andronicus was a foreigner, moreover a freed slave, with deficient knowledge of Latin, and though he probably wrote and acted his plays only as a means of livelihood, the Romans immediately laid down their arms, and throughout the following century their dramatic repertoire came to consist almost exclusively of imita-tions from Greek models, whether they chose to adopt the original subjects and figures, or tried to fill them with fresh blood by adapting the Greek form to the treatment of Roman subjects. The national popular farces were maintained merely as after-plays to the

imported artistic dramas, and now they were not committed to writing.

Tragedy was represented by a number of names,
such as Nævius, the immediate successor of Andronicus ; Ennius, the adapter of Euripides, who also wrote
tragedies on Roman subjects, the so - called *fabulæ
prætextæ*, *i.e.* plays performed in Roman costume, like
the *Rape of the Sabine Women* ; the painter Pacuvius,
nephew of Ennius, who won great fame by his plays ;
Accius, Atilius, also a clever dramatist, and Asinius
Pollio ; finally, in the time of the Empire, the well-known
tragedies of Seneca, which probably were only meant for
reading : they were never performed. The latter interest
us in so far as they became the prototypes of the first
attempts made by the Renaissance to introduce the
"classical" drama. After all, the list of tragic authors
is not imposing ; we know at most thirty-six authors and
one hundred and fifty pieces, and of these none but the
plays of Seneca are extant.

In the way of repertoire the Roman tragedy does not
offer any interest beyond what is known from the Greek.
The forms of the two are essentially alike, only in the
Roman the part of the chorus is reduced to the
narrowest limits possible. The types of character are
also the same, but the dialogue is more solemn and
bombastic, compensating for its lack of deeper feeling
by exaggerated imagery. At the time of Cicero tragedies
were divided into three acts, afterwards into five.

Comedy also derives its materials partly from
Greek subjects (*fabula palliata*), partly from national
sources (*fabula togata*). In the former case it is the

later Attic Comedy which is imitated or translated. The Aristophanic Comedy was too thoroughly Greek, too local to allow of its being transplanted to the Latin stage. Even the later Attic Comedy had peculiar characteristics which ill harmonised with Roman customs. Thus the cunning slave who moves the wheel of the action, and the familiar relation in which he stands to his master, were quite alien to Roman notions. Nevertheless this character constantly appeared in the repertoire, and came down to our own time in the shape of Scapin or Henrik (Holberg). Nor is it at all a Roman feature to allow the *hetaira* to occupy such an important place in the comedy as she does in the Greek drama. Therefore in the *togata*, the comedies with Roman subjects, these figures are pushed into the background, whereas the family, especially its female elements, are much more prominent than in the *palliata.* Otherwise these two kinds of plays were nearly alike in form, and this form again was that of the Attic comedy. Both were written in verse, and not divided into acts. Even prologue and epilogue were adopted. The latter, however, was frequently reduced to the brief *plaudite !* (applaud !).

The two names which tower above those of all other Latin playwrights are Plautus and Terence; both are representatives of *fabula palliata* (comedy imitated from the Greek) ; otherwise they differ very much. Plautus is a coarse popular poet, a practical stage-manager who knows what kind of entertainment pleases the majority of the public. In broad and rapid features and with inexhaustible humour he develops his simple intrigue.

Being himself a man of the people, he had experienced the vicissitudes of life, had been high up and low down, so he knew how to "manage" his public. Born in Umbria about 254 B.C. in a humble condition, he went at a very early age to the theatre to earn his living. In this situation he succeeded in making a comfortable fortune, which he invested in commercial business. By these transactions he lost all, and had to take service in a mill until his adaptations of Greek plays, especially those of Menander, Diphilus and Philemon put him on his feet again. He died in the year 184 B.C. In spite of numerous examples of bad taste, of improbability and carelessness of form, there is a liveliness and spirit in his plays, which not only testify to the excellence of his models, but also entitle him to rank high as a comic author (fig. 57).

Molière is indebted to him for his *Amphitryon* and his *Avare*, and Holberg's *Abracadabra* is neither more nor less than a translation (in many places almost literal) of his *Mostellaria* ("the Ghost-story"). Long after his death his plays kept their place on the stage, and were constantly enjoyed by the crowd ; at the same time he came to be acknowledged as a classical author by the learned authorities.

Terence is not, and does not pretend to be, anything but a mere translator. It is true, he tampers a little with the originals, adding or omitting a trifle here and there, but his adaptations do not bear any independent personal stamp, not even the prologues which are composed by himself and are of an entirely polemic character. He was a careful, elegant translator of the admired Greeks,

57

58

57—Plautine types. The swaggering soldier and the parasite. The two figures
at the sides represent the theatre-police with their staves.

58—Scene from a Roman comedy.

which caused Cæsar to call him "half a Menander," but
scarcely more.   He died young—in the year 159 B.C.—
and only six of his plays were acted.¹   Titles and names,
as well as the whole tone of the plays of Terence, are
perfectly Greek, though perhaps a little more polished
than the originals.   While Plautus is not afraid of representing the *hetairai* as grasping, business-like prostitutes,
in Terence these women are almost as pure as the sweet-
hearts in our own vaudevilles.   The plot is woven with
the most ingenious minuteness and solved with much
greater consistency than in Plautus.   Therefore we read
Terence with great pleasure, but we cannot help sus-
pecting that his elegance was a little too refined for a
Roman audience.   In the prologue to his " Mother-in-
Law " he complains in a playful manner that formerly
his art struggled in vain against rope-dancers and boxers,
and he solicits the attention of the public with insinuat-
ing words (fig. 58).

This, however, may only have been a sign that on
the whole the interest of the people in higher dramatic
art was in the decline.   And indeed, after the death of
Terence taste steadily deteriorated.   While the desire
for luxury and outward comfort increased, the taste for
good old simple comedy gradually disappeared, and at
last was entirely blunted by performances in the circus,
by driving matches, at which—as at our modern races and
sporting competitions—passionate gambling formed the
principal attraction, and by the immense moral corruption
to which mere dramas did not offer sufficient excitement.

¹ *Andria, The Eunuch, Heauton timoroumenos* (" the Self-tormentor"),
Phormio, Hekyra (" the Mother-in-law "), and *Adelphi* (" the Brothers ").

At the time of the Empire the people no longer cared to see the old tragedies and comedies. Though the admission was free, the places stood empty when Plautus and Terence were acted, whereas the people rushed to see *Mimes* and *Atellanae*, which in former times had only been interludes or after-plays to the more valuable dramas, but which now, owing to the caprice of a depraved taste, were placed in the front rank, though in a somewhat different form.

We have already touched upon the origin of the *Atellanae*. From being popular farces performed in the streets by young Roman citizens, they now appeared on the boards and were played by professional actors. They still preserved their character of low comical and partly improvised art, though the fashion of the time raised them to the level of a branch of literature. The *Atellanae* became direct forerunners of the *commedia dell' arte*, afterwards so important in Italy, and its recognised masks have indeed survived to our own days. Four of these figures were the chief supports of the whole slender action, four types which still bore the stamp of their Oscan origin.[1]

Maccus (fig. 59) was the foolish country lad—coarse, stupid, impudent and greedy—who was always taken in and always got the blows : the prototype of Pulcinella in the *commedia dell' arte*. He was represented with a low, flat forehead, a big head, a monstrous nose, which drooped down on his mouth, and a double hunch on his back. His garment was made of white wool. Bucco (fig. 60) was the stupid, jabbering and impudent fool,

---

[1] Atella was Oscan.

a swaggering parasite who readily swallows the worst insults if they are accompanied by a dainty bit. Pappus ("daddy") was the ridiculous old miser, always convinced of his own skill, and always dragged into the worst adventures; in love with and deceived by all women : the prototype of Pantalone in the *commedia dell' arte*. Finally *Dossennus*, about whom we possess but little trustworthy information, ready for all knavish tricks and disguises in order to get money from old Daddy, and therefore appearing as miracle doctor, soothsayer, etc. ; *il dottore* of the comedy of masks.

However, one of the principal attractions of the *Atellanae* consisted in the personal attacks with which they were always flavoured. Not even the emperor got off scot free. Thus at the time when Tiberius was living at Capri, an allusion to the life of the old "buck" was greeted with a storm of applause. Under Nero an *Atellanae* - player, Datus, accompanied the sentences : " All hail to you, Father ! All hail to you, Mother ! " with gestures which indicated that the emperor had poisoned Claudius and attempted to drown Agrippina. Sometimes the bold comedians escaped alive from their venture, but at any rate it increased the excitement of the public to know that life was at stake. Thus Caligula ordered an actor to be publicly burned in the amphitheatre for a similar ambiguous allusion.

Of the Mimes only a few unimportant fragments remain, but all contemporary reports testify to the fact that they were inconceivably obscene and sensual. It was natural, therefore, that they should have become the favourite performances of the period of decay. In its lowest form the Roman *mimus* confined itself to the imitation of the cries of animals. Afterwards it developed into imitations of erotic situations by gestures, accompanied by burlesque grimaces and coarse jokes. But at the time of the Empire it grew into real comedy of a much more artistic stamp than the *Atellanae*. The fool in these farces was named Sannio (fig. 61). No masks were used, and neither *cothurnus* nor *soccus* (the low shoe used in comedy). Therefore the mime-players or mimes (the actors were called so as well as the plays) had the surname of *planipedes*, the flat-footed. Their costume was a kind of gaudy harlequin jacket (*centunculus*), and their heads were clean shaven. The mimes were the only kind of plays in which women were allowed to perform, which perhaps was one of their great attractions.

In these pieces dances were inserted which were always of a very obscene nature. The whole—literally whole—costume of the dancing women consisted of a short thin under-garment (fig. 62). On certain occasions, as the *floralia* (spring festivals), every excess was allowed, and the public used to request that the dancers should take off even this remnant of a cover. On such occasions, however, decent people left the theatre before the excesses began, and we quite understand Cicero's reproaching himself bitterly for having assisted at the performance of mimes.

In spite of their bad repute the mime-actors were admitted to the parties of the most distinguished Romans. Sulla as well as Antonius who, it is true, did not win their fame by their virtuous lives, had constant and

59

60

61

61

62

59—Maccus.   60—Bucco.   61—Popular types of fools.

62—Mime-dancer.

intimate intercourse with mimes.   It caused great and
scandalous sensation that in his public journeys undertaken for the purpose of stirring up the people in Cæsar's
favour, Antonius travelled all round Italy with Cytheris,
the mime-dancer, at his side in the same sedan-chair.

II

THE THEATRE

The Plain Forms of the First Play Houses in Rome—Democratic Equality
in the Distribution of the Places—Permanent Theatres in Rome—
Development of the Roman Theatres from the Greek—The Raised
Stage—Temporary Theatres—Immense Luxury of Equipment—
Mechanical Feats.

THE first period of theatrical performance in Rome
exhibits a simplicity, nay a poverty, which does not give
the faintest suspicion of the extravagant luxury of later
times.   In the interval between the first appearance of
Andronicus (240 B.C.) and 174 B.C., there was practically
no theatre in Rome.   For each festival at which
plays were performed, a wooden *skênê* was improvised,
in front of which the play was acted, while it was left
to the spectators themselves to provide seats by bringing
with them forms and chairs for the occasion.   Even as
late as the year 194 B.C., the democratic people was discontented and scandalised at finding that seats were
reserved for the senators apart from the remainder of
the audience.   In 174 B.C. the censors erected the first
skênê (*scæna*) of *stone*, while the auditorium (*cavea*) still

continued to be provisional; and in every case, if the spectators wanted to sit, they had to bring their own chairs.   In 185 B.C. it was even forbidden to sit down during the performance.   Not till fourteen years after the death of Terence, in 145 B.C., after the time of the classical drama, was the first complete theatre built after the Greek fashion with terrace-shaped tiers surrounding an *orchêstra*.   But this theatre also was only of wood. It was Pompey who built the first Roman stone theatre, which was finished in 55 B.C.   Two more permanent theatres were built in Rome, one by Cornelius Balbus, the other by Marcellus; both were finished in the year 13 B.C.   Rome never had more than these three permanent theatres; but during the Empire temporary play-houses were constantly erected, which in size and magnificence were by no means inferior to the stone theatres.   The latter were indeed comparatively small. While the amphitheatre, where fights of gladiators and of animals took place, had room for 87,000 people, the Balbus-theatre only held 11,510, the Pompey-theatre 17,580, and the Marcellus-theatre 20,500.

The Roman theatre was built after the Hellenic-Greek pattern, but in being transplanted to the Italian soil, the latter underwent some alterations which became of considerable importance, also, to the theatrical architecture of later times.   Of particular importance was the introduction of an elevated *podium*, a permanent platform (*logeion*), on which the action was represented, as thereby the Roman theatre became the pattern of our modern stage-building.   This raised platform developed quite naturally out of the Greek scenic arrangement, and simply conformed itself to the requirements of certain changes in taste and in dramatic literature.

What had happened in Greece was this : by degrees, as the dances and songs of the chorus no longer formed the central part of the dramatic action, and as the chorus had to content itself more and more with being merely the companion of the principal characters and a (frequently) superfluous interpreter of the author, the action imperceptibly retired up to the *proskênion* wall, from behind which the principal persons came out and through which they retired. In Rome, where the chorus was either quite abolished or merely kept up as a survival from Greek originals, without having any traditional or national importance, of course it became useless to assign such large dimensions to the circular dancing-place, the *orchêstra*. At the same time the plays lost their purely religious character, and therefore the altar no longer retained its importance as the permanent centre of the action. The later Attic Comedy and after it Plautus and Terence, with their pictures of life in the streets, of everyday people and of domestic intrigues, demand a nearer approach to reality in the scenic arrangements. Estrades, stairs, pillars are erected, benches, chairs, etc., are placed according to the requirements of the piece, and all these accessories are naturally brought into close contact with the *proskênion* wall, which now becomes the permanent background of the action, while formerly it only occasionally served as such. So the extent of the stage was limited to the half of the *orchêstra* which was nearest to the *proskênion*.

The other half was appropriated by the public, to which it offered the best places for seeing what passed close up to the *skênê*.   In Rome it was here that places were assigned to the senators, the foreign ambassadors, the aediles and similar dignitaries.   The old auditorium was cut down to a semi-circle to make it easier for all spectators to see the performance.   In order to separate the actor more distinctly from the audience, the part of the *orchêstra* which was now used by spectators, was lowered some feet, whereas the *paraskênia*, the outer wings of the *skênê*, were advanced in order to produce side walls, and thus the transformation to the Roman theatre with its elevated *podium* or stage was effected.

The annexed diagrams give a graphic representation of the development described above.   Fig. 63 represents a section of a typical Greek theatre.   To the right we see the auditorium, the circular form of the *orchêstra* or *konistra* is indicated by a dotted semi-circle; the roof of the *proskênion* is marked as *theo-logeion*, because as a matter of fact, the deities spoke from thence; between the *proskênion* and the auditorium appears the entrance gate, *parodos*.

Fig. 64 is a section of a typical Roman theatre, such as is found in Pompeii or in the reconstructed Greek theatres.   Here we see how the bottom of the *orchêstra*, the *konistra*, is lowered some feet; the auditorium descends to the new ground-level.   Thus the stage is raised in the same proportion; the former circumference of the *orchêstra* is still indicated by a dotted semi-circle in order to show the width of the piece cut off.

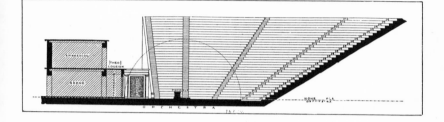

63

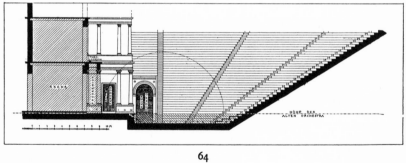

64

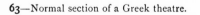

63—Normal section of a Greek theatre.   64—Normal section of a Roman theatre.

The old entrance gates now led to the stage
(*logeion*); therefore new entrances were arranged for
the public through vaulted passages beneath the auditorium leading to the *orchêstra*.   Fig. 65 shows one
of the best preserved Roman theatres—the theatre in
Orange (Southern France).   The last illustration is a
reconstruction.

Most of the Roman theatres were open to the sky;
the stage only was frequently roofed (comp. fig. 65); but
the Romans of the later Republic and of the Empire,
who were more effeminate than the Greeks, spread
enormous awnings over the auditorium; it was, moreover, provided with aqueducts which refreshed the air
by constantly watering the passages.   During the
Empire, not only water, but a mixture of wine, water
and crocus juice was conducted by pressure up to the
highest tiers, whence a delicate, fragrant rain was
diffused over the theatre in the finest jets.

Gradually an incredible luxury developed itself in
the decoration of the playhouse.   Even the permanent
theatres were magnificent enough ; marble, gold, beautiful statues, expensive woven carpets, vied with each
other in charming the eye.   But the temporary theatres
far surpassed these permanent resorts of art, and fortunes
were squandered in order to satisfy the caprices of a few
months.   The performances, being open to the public
free of charge, were not pecuniary enterprises; they
were gifts to the people from the ruler of the state,
or from some rich man who wished to gain popularity
and glory.   The luxury which was lavished on these
ephemeral buildings is almost inconceivable, even to

our modern notions.   Take, for instance, the theatre
which the ædile Aemilius Scaurus had erected ; its
skêne consisted of three storeys each with its colonnade ; the lowest had pillars of marble, the middle one
pillars of glass (the most expensive material of the
time), and the uppermost pillars of gilt wood.   There
were altogether 360 pillars, and between them stood
3000 magnificent statues.   The auditorium held 80,000
persons, and, like the stage, was beautifully decorated
with pictures and purple carpets.   The donor, we must
say, was scarcely as liberal to his slaves as to the
Roman people, for in their fury against him they set
fire to this wonderful colossal wooden theatre, thereby
causing their master a loss of one hundred million
sestertii (more than eight hundred thousand pounds).

Another remarkable theatre was erected in the year
53 by Scribonius Curio on the occasion of his father's
funeral.   In the morning there were two wooden
theatres, each with its stage, on which plays were
performed.   The theatres turned their circular backs
towards each other, so that the sounds from the
one did not disturb the performance in the other.
When the performance was ended, while all the
spectators were still seated in their places, the two
auditoriums were suddenly turned round so as to fit
together and form a circus, an amphitheatre, which
was immediately made ready for warlike games.   Pliny,
who describes both these theatres, is shocked at the
recklessness with which Curio risked the lives and
limbs of his fellow-citizens.   However, we do not hear
that the experiment failed, and modern engineers

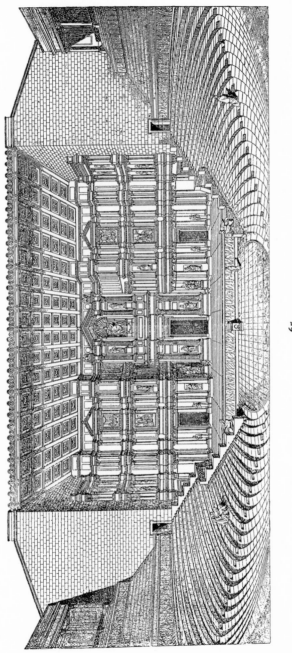

65

65—The theatre in Orange (reconstructed).

really think that this piece of technical skill may have
been practicable even at that time. The spreading
of the immense awning is considered as an almost
equally remarkable testimony to the high state of
perfection of the architectural skill of that period. They
are said to have employed sailors to set it.

Curtains also (*aulæa*) were used in the Roman
theatres in contrast with the Greek, though probably only
in those which were covered with a roof like the little
one in Pompeii. However, the curtain was not dropped
from above as in our theatres, where all draperies are
kept in a loft for scenic machinery, but it was hidden
in a groove along the front border of the stage, and
raised at the close of the play.

As to the distribution of the places, it has been
already stated that the senators occupied the seats in the
earlier *orchêstra*; otherwise the arrangement was less
democratic than in Greece. The fourteen front rows—
subsellia—behind the senators were reserved for the
knights ; even the common people were seated according
to their rank, and the lowest were confined to the
uppermost places. The places which ranked highest
were the so-called *tribunalia*, a sort of boxes above the
entrance to the *orchêstra*, one on each side of the stage.
In one of the *tribunalia* the Emperor and the donor of
the play were seated, in the other the Vestals, and
among them the Empress. This distribution of the
places was established in the time of Augustus, but
remained almost unaltered throughout the whole period
of the Empire. The places were divided into wedge-
shaped parts, *cunei*, exactly corresponding to the Greek

kerkides, and the tickets of admission were marked with
the figure of the *cuneus* or *kerkis*, to which the ticket
gave admission.

III

THE ACTORS

Social Position and Administrative Conditions of the Actors—The Roman
Public—Claqueurs—Quintus Roscius Gallus and his Importance to
Dramatic Art—Æsopus—Decline of Dramatic Art—Singing introduced as a Separate Performance in the Drama—Pantomime super-
sedes real Dramatic Art.

THE common denomination of Roman actors was the
word *histrio*, but each separate class had its particular
name besides.   That of the comic actor was *comœdus*,
the tragedian was called *tragœdus*, the mime, *mimus*, and
the pantomime-player—whose speciality we are going to
describe more in detail—*pantomimus*.   The Romans did
not, like the Greeks, content themselves with three
permanent actors paid by the State;   each piece—
tragedy, comedy or mime—required a whole company,
grex or *caterva*.   Such a company was hired or paid by
the magistrate who supplied the entertainment, and at
the head of the company stood a manager, *dominus
gregis* or *actor*.   The director of a troop of mimes was
called *archimimus*, and his company also included female
performers, *mimæ*, whereas in all other classes of acting
the female parts were always performed by men.

The position of professional actors at Rome was as
miserable and despised as it had been respected and
estimable in Greece ;   or rather, at Rome actors had no

position at all, for no Roman citizen could adopt the stage as a means of livelihood without losing all his civic privileges. Dramatic art was imported into Italy by Greek slaves; to the Romans this imported amusement was not connected with anything sacred; there was no festal and noble contest which might have tempted them to exercise this art, which they saw slaves and freed mèn perform as a miserable means of gaining their living. No wonder, therefore, that not only the social position of the actors was low (it was so already from the reason that only the lowest members of society cultivated dramatic art), but that their legal position was also of such a nature that no citizen who had any reputation to lose could condescend to appear as a paid actor on the stage.

The whole class was under the ban of infamy. The Prætorian Edict stigmatised certain classes as disreputable; for instance, deserters, panders, thieves, robbers, and all those who mounted the boards as actors or reciters.[1] In consequence of this infamy an actor was excluded from all public functions and honours and from military service, and if an actor or an actor's son married the child, grandchild or great-grandchild of a senator, the marriage might be declared invalid. A husband who discovered his wife in the act of betraying him with an actor, was allowed to kill the latter if he caught him in his own house. A soldier who appeared on the stage was instantly punished with death.

We can understand that none but slaves who were

---

[1] Comp. Max Burchard: *Das Recht der Schauspieler*, Stuttgart, 1896, p. 8 and note 16.

brought up and trained for the purpose of procuring glory and honour for their master, could attach themselves to an art which entailed so much shame.   Though, as a rule, the manager was an actor himself, and as such subject to the same infamy as his subordinates, he had almost power of life and limb over them, and flogged them mercilessly if they committed any fault during the performance.[1]   The public was much more exacting and regardless of the actors than in Greece.   The women talked loudly and laughed during the performances, the children who were brought by their nurses cried and screamed, and people did not mind coming late ; they were shown to their seats by the functionaries without heeding what was passing on the stage.   By-and-by companies of *claqueurs* were organised which were engaged by different parties and tried to outbid each other in violent manifestations of opinion, frequently causing the greatest tumults and scandals, especially during the Empire, when the differences of opinion not unfrequently degenerated into bloody fights and murders. Under such circumstances, however, the public suffered more than the actors ; but on less stormy days as well the people were very easily excited.   Cicero relates[2] how the slightest offence against the rules might become fatal to an actor.   A wrong quantity of a syllable was sufficient to make the whole audience shout and hiss furiously.

In spite of the general contempt with which actors as a class were regarded, the individual dramatic per-

---

[1] Comp., *e.g.*, the epilogue of Plautus's *The Box* : " He who has made a mistake is flogged, he who has made none drinks."

[2] Cicero : *Parad.* iii. 2.

former frequently succeeded in rising above his colleagues and in gaining wealth as well as consideration. More than any other the famous actor Roscius contributed to raise the standard of his class. He was, it is true, originally a slave like most of his comrades, and was not called Roscius till after he had been freed. This name, which afterwards became synonymous with a great actor, was that of his master. His full name was Quintus Roscius Gallus.

No other Roman player obtained popularity and esteem equal to his. He was a comic actor and possessed a power over the public which was simply astounding. The favour in which he stood was even transferred to his pupils, and any one whom he protected was pretty sure of future success on the boards. Roscius himself might even play less well without incurring the displeasure of the public. If for once he happened to be less successful than usual, people only said: " He *would* not play," or "he was not quite well." Part of his outward circumstances we know from a speech made in his defence by no less a person than Cicero, on the occasion of his suit against one Fannius Chærea, whose slave, Panurgus, Roscius had instructed. Among other things we are informed of his colossal income. His salary for one performance was 1000 denarii (about £31), and during his maturity his annual income amounted to about 500,000 sestertii (more than £4425). However, he was anything but grasping; and next to his art, his noble, honest character went far to raise his class to a higher position in the general esteem. For a long time after having gained a considerable fortune and as early as ten years before the law-suit conducted for him by Cicero, he acted without remuneration.   Sulla appreciated him highly and bestowed the golden ring upon him, by which he was raised to the rank of a senator.

The art of Roscius kept decidedly aloof from the method of the earlier period.   The principal aim of the first Roman actors had been to gain ground, to find an open ear for their art.   But the refined Greek method of acting was incomprehensible to the Roman public, which demanded coarser food; the comedy, therefore, resorted to coarse jokes, tasteless fighting scenes, overdrawn caricatures, the tragedy to bombastic, exaggerated acting. Great honour is due to Roscius for having placed artistic *moderation* in the front rank, for having followed it as his leading principle, and for having impressed on the public that the highest art lies here, and not in the clown-like exaggeration which had been in favour hitherto.   His diction as well as his gesticulation remained unsurpassed on account of its graceful yet truly comic power; and Cicero himself, who cannot find adequate words to commend the noble art of Roscius, admits having learned much from his technique, which he had introduced into his own rhetoric.   Roscius died about the year 62 B.C.

A contemporary of his was Æsopus, the tragedian, who in his line obtained almost as great fame as Roscius in his, and gained equally colossal sums by his performances.   But he did not possess the moderation of Roscius, either as a man or as an artist.   He was a great spendthrift, and it is he of whom it is told that

in order to form an approximate idea of the taste of the
human tongue, he ordered a dish to be prepared of the
tongues of rare singing and screeching birds.   In spite
of his extravagance he left a large fortune.   His best
parts were Atreus in the tragedy of Accius, the title
character in the *Andromache* of Ennius, and Aga-
memnon in the *Iphigenia* of the same author.   He is
blamed for not having left off acting in time.   He lived
longer than Roscius, but on the death of the latter his
flourishing period was over.   Cicero appreciated him
highly, and the actor did not betray the friendship of
the great orator, but proved devoted and grateful to
him during his exile.

These two prominent actors naturally founded
schools ; the good style they had created survived
till the early years of the Empire, and formed the
climax of Roman dramatic art.   Their art was based
in the main on the best Greek mode of representation
and differed from it only in details.   The actors of
this period frequently, but not always, used masks,
unlike the older Roman generation, which only used
wigs and paint.   Formerly it was only Atellanian
amateur actors who were allowed to hide their heads
with a mask, but the increased consideration which
Roscius and Æsopus gained for scenic artists caused
this privilege (for as such the right of wearing masks
was considered) to be extended to actors as well.   It
might still happen that the public—if it wanted to deal
a hard blow at an actor—ordered him to take off his
mask and show his face on the open stage, by which it
was intended to remind him of his ignominious social

position.   Of course such an insult was deeply felt by
the actor.   The costume was a direct imitation of the
Greek, with the sole exception that plays treating of
Roman subjects were acted in ordinary Roman dress.

As to the mode of delivery, the feature in which
the Roman fashion differed most from the Greek was
the much more independent position it gave to song.
Whereas in Greece, song, musical declamation and ordinary speech were mixed up together in so far all three
modes of expression were constantly employed by the
same actor, this was not the case in Rome.   Here the
lyric parts, *cantica*, required a special vocal training and
peculiar natural gifts, which most frequently necessitated
that these parts—though this was fatal to all illusion—
should be executed by a professional singer, *cantor*,
while the part of the actor was reduced to the making
of the appropriate gestures.   During the time of the
Empire this opera-like element was gradually eliminated
from tragedy — as a matter of course it was chiefly
tragedy which contained musical parts — and came
to constitute independent performances in which the
singer—either alone or together with the chorus—acted
certain favourite effective scenes in the current dramas.
It was in this kind of dramatic performance that the
Emperor Nero was fond of appearing.   Suetonius tells
us that he performed long tragic scenes under cover of
a mask representing such characters as Orestes the
matricide, the blinded Œdipus, the mad Hercules, etc.
He also appeared in female parts, for which he used to
have his masks painted and modelled after the ladies
who for the time being possessed his favour.   It was

his passion for this semi-dramatic kind of performance which in his hour of death made him utter the well-known words : "What an artist the world loses in me!"

Of even much greater and more fatal importance to dramatic art than the elimination of song from the drama, was the establishment of *gesture*—the so-called *panto-mimus*—as an independent art. Actors and orators in Rome had constantly practised the art of gesture with great zeal, and had reached a perfection of which now-a-days we can scarcely form a clear idea. To this day the Italians are famous for their particularly expressive and distinct gestures. The language of their hands contains a number of half symbolic, half descriptive movements, which to us slow northern people often produce the effect of a complete system of language for the deaf and dumb. We are scarcely mistaken in considering this highly developed power of gesture as a feeble remnant of the study which for centuries the ancient Romans devoted to the expressive move-ments of the hands and other parts of the body. During the Empire, indeed, pantomime became the favourite branch of the drama, and nearly supplanted the spoken drama.

The Roman pantomime, however, was by no means the same kind of thing as the mimic representation by a whole company of ballet-dancers which we call by that name. By the word *pantomimus* the Romans understood the mimic, or rather plastic performance by which an artist interpreted a dramatic subject by his movements. This speciality was developed to its full glory under Augustus, particularly by the two famous pantomimes—the actors were called pantomimes as well as the art they cultivated—Pylades from Cilicia, and Bathyllus from Alexandria, and these two artists remained the noblest, and at the same time the most prominent, though far from the only representatives, of this new form of art.

The subjects of the pantomimes were mostly drawn from well-known tragedies, especially from those which embodied legends of Greek mythology; but on the whole, no historical subject was considered beyond their province. To the performance belonged a written text, which was sung, in the earliest times by a singer, after-wards—an improvement introduced by Pylades—by a chorus; and the mimic action was accompanied by a whole orchestra consisting of flutes, shields and cymbals, cithern and lyre. The rhythm was accented by peculiar percussion instruments, *scabilla*, a kind of cymbal, which were fastened to the ankles, and which, when the legs were moved, clashed against each other with shrill sounds.[1] The dancer or mimic, whichever we like to call him, represented successively the principal persons under different costumes, and described by his movements only (his face was hidden by a mask which—unlike that of the drama—had its mouth closed) all situations and feelings with a truth and perspicuity which inspired even experts with the highest admiration. The pantomimes did not even recoil from highly tragic subjects such as Atreus and Thyestes, the mad Ajax, the raging Hercules, Niobe, Hector, etc. But the most favoured subjects were the

[1] Comp. Friedlaender : *Darst. aus d. Sittengeschichte Roms.*, 6 Aufl., ii. p. 453.

myths which offered opportunities for picturing amorous situations, in which branch Bathyllus was the first to distinguish himself, and in which afterwards, under Nero, Paris, the favourite of this emperor, won his fame. Such subjects as Venus and Mars in the net of Vulcan, Leda with the Swan, Danae and the Golden Shower, Venus and Adonis, Apollo and Daphne, were constant favourites in the pantomimic repertoire.

This remarkable branch of art was of too great importance and exercised an effect too strong, even on critical and sensible men, to allow us to doubt that it contained a strong element of genuine art. Perhaps it is to it that we must trace the particular Italian gift of dramatic representation. Lucian, who was certainly not deficient in critical power, describes the effect of the pantomime in these strong words : " It touches, charms and *instructs*. The play reveals the interior man with such truthfulness and depth that we have the greatest pleasure in recognising ourselves in it, and think we have accomplished the task imposed by the Delphic god."[1] This newly-created form of art seemed to contain so much energy and truth that it completely overshadowed dramatic art, which was gradually stagnating in dead and stereotyped forms. Even the most rebellious had to give in. The well-known cynic philosopher, Demetrius, who lived under Nero, continued for a long time to speak depreciatingly of pantomimic art ; he maintained in particular that the *pantomimus* could not create anything himself, but had to depend entirely on the choral songs and the music.

[1] " Know thyself" was the motto of the Delphic oracle.

So Paris, the most famous *pantomimus* of his time,
vowed to convert the inflexible philosopher from his
heresies, and invited him to be present at a performance
in which, without any support of text or music, he
represented the guilty love of Mars and Venus.
Now, according to Lucian, he expressed merely by
dumb show the jealous anger of Vulcan, the catching of
the lovers in the invisible net, the amusement of the
other gods who were called to see, the shame of Venus
and the entreaties of Mars, all in such a wonderfully
true and comprehensive manner, that the cynic was
compelled to give up his former opinion and to admit
that he had been unjust to pantomimic art.

During the Empire there arose a frantic enthusiasm
for pantomimes, especially among the higher classes.
The people at large found the unveiled coarseness and
levity of the mimes more to their taste. But the truly
artistic element contained in pantomime, combined
with the increasing lubricity of its matter, was just
the *raffinement* required for throwing the enervated
Roman aristocracy into raptures. Here they had a
spicy extract of the boldest subjects served in an
artistic, or at least a masterly way. Beautiful bodies in
magnificent garments exhibited to the fastidious public
in plastic forms the heroes and gods, about whose
sufferings they no longer cared to hear through the too
deep words of the great poets. Why listen to the long-
winded sentences of a Sophocles when Bathyllus could
express the same emotions as comprehensively by some
twists of his body? There arose special branches
within the pantomime, as, *e.g.*, the peculiar draping-

dance, the point of which was that the dancer should make his or her garment form different figures, such as that of a swan, the hair of Venus, etc., after the fashion of the modern "serpentine dance" invented by Loïe Fuller, or like the plastic draping-performances of the last century, in which some ladies, *e.g.* Händel-Schütz and Emma Hart, the mistress of Lord Hamilton, excelled.

However, what became to an ever-increasing degree the chief attraction of the pantomimes was the living pictures of amorous scenes which, though carried to the utmost limits of boldness, were represented with so much elegance, grace and flexibility, combined with perfect control of the body, that they formed the favourite entertainment of Roman ladies. Under Nero the enthusiasm for these dances rose to a perfectly fanatical cult. The emperor compelled distinguished Romans to dance pantomimes, and he himself appeared before them in such performances. His court-dancer was the above-mentioned Paris, who was also his best and most intimate friend. More intimate still were the relations between the younger Paris and the Empress Domitia, a favour, however, which cost the poor pantomime his life. It is a well-known fact that Justinian married Theodora, one of the most shameless and immoral dancing women ; and when during the reigns of Constantine and Galerius there was danger of famine, all orators, poets, philosophers, learned men and teachers were driven out of the town, but three thousand dancers were allowed to remain : rather go a little more hungry than dispense with the best amusement !

No wonder that Christians turned their sharpest weapons against this madness. Augustine was of opinion that the invention of this kind of plays was due to the wickedness of evil spirits who, having foreseen that the circus-mania would stop some day, had sent this much more destructive disease into the world in order to give even greater joy to the devil. And indeed, at this period pantomime was nothing but an indecent means of stimulating the senses, a pretext for satisfying corrupt desires. Dramatic art had died long ago, the bizarre caprices of Pylades and Bathyllus were its last flicker. Now Christianity drove its stake through this antique spectre, and ancient dramatic art ended its existence with a hideous lascivious grimace.

BIBLIOGRAPHY

Waitz: Antropologie der Naturvölker, Bd. I—VI.

Klein, J. L.: Geschichte des Dramas, Bd. I—III.

Edèlestand du Méril: La Comédie ancienne, Bd. I—II.

Bahnson, Kr.: Etnografien fremstillet i dens Hovedtræk. Kbhvn. 1894. Bd. I—II.

Henningsen, J.: Det himmelske Rige. Kbhvn. 1887.

Doolittle, Justus: Social Life of the Chinese. London, 1868.

Forbes, F. E.: Five Years in China. London, 1848.

Timkowski, G.: Reise nach China durch d. Mongoley. A. d. Russ. v. J. A. C. Schmidt. Bd. I—III.

Ampère, J.-J.: Du Théâtre chinois (Revue d. d. Mondes, 15. sept. 1838).

Bousquet, Georges: Le Théâtre au Japon (Rev. d. d. Mondes, 15. août 1814).

Schroeder, Leop. v.: Indiens Literatur und Cultur. Leipzig, 1887.

Max Müller: India, what can it teach us? London, 1883.

Lévi, Sylvain: Le Théâtre indien. Paris, 1890.

Senart, Emile: Le Théâtre indien (Rev. d. d. Mondes, 1 Mai 1891).

Meier, Ernst: Sakuntala (Introduction).

Hammerich, M.: Sakuntala (Introduction). K. 1858.

Brandes, Edv.: Lervognen (Introduction).

Bernhardy: Grundriss der griechischen Literatur, Bd. I—II.

Croiset, A. & M.: Histoire de la Littérature grecque, t. III. Paris, 1891.

Bernhardy: Grundriss der römischen Literatur. 5te Bearbeitung. Braunschweig, 1872.

Donaldson: The Theatre of the Greeks. Cambridge, 1860.

Teuffel, W. S.: Geschichte der römischen Literatur. 5te Aufl. Leipzig, 1890.

Friedländer, L.: Darstellungen aus der Sittengeschichte Roms. 6te Aufl. 1889.

Marquardt, J.: Römische Staatsalterthümer. Bd. III. 2te Aufl. 1885.

Jung, Jul.: Leben und Sitten der Römer in der Kaiserzeit. Prag, 1883. Bd. I—III.

Blümner, H.: Leben und Sitten der Griechen. Leipz. 1887.

Wieseler: Theatergebäude und Denkmäler der Griechen.

Ussing, J. L.: Den yngre attiske Komedie. K. 1875.

    „   Scenica, filologisk-archæologiske Betragtninger. K. 1897.

Duruy, V.: Le Théâtre d'Athènes au Ve siècle (R. d. d. M., oct. 1886).

240 BIBLIOGRAPHY

Lüders, O.: Die dionysischen Künstler. Berlin, 1873.

Poland, Franciskus: De collegiis artificum Dionysiacorum. Dresden, 1895.

Baumeister: Denkmäler des klassichen Alterthums. Bd. I—IV.

Oehmichen, G.: Bühnenwesen der Griechen und Römer. (I. *Iw. Müllers* Handbuch der klass. Alterthumswissenschaft, Bd. V, 3 Abtn. München, 1890.)

Stengel, Paul: Die griechishen Sakralalterthümer. (München.)

Müller, Albert: Lehrbuch der griechischen Bühnenalterthümer. Freiburg, 1886.

Haigh, A. E.: The Attic Theatre. Oxford, 1889.

Wilamowitz-Möllendorf: Die Bühne des Aeschylos. (I. "Hermes," XXI.)

Capps, Edward: Vitruvius and the Greek Stage. (I. "Studies in Classical Philology," I.)

Bursian, Konrad: Schauspieler und Schauspielkunst im griechischen Altherthum. (" Riehl's hist. Taschenbuch," 5te Folge. 1875.)

Opitz, Richard: Schauspiel und Theaterwesen der Griechen und Römer. Leipzig, 1889.

Bethe, E.: Prolegomena zur Geschichte des Theaters im Altherthum. Leipz. 1896.

Dörpfeld, W. &> Emil Reisch: Das griechische Theater. Athen u. Leipzig, 1896.

INDEX